AUTISM

PARENT TO PARENT

Sanity-Saving Advice for Every Parent with a Child on the Autism Spectrum

SHANNON PENROD

Host Of *Autism Live*, The #1 Rated Autism Podcast Worldwide

Foreword by Dr. Doreen Granpeesheh

ADVANCE PRAISE FOR
AUTISM: PARENT TO PARENT

"Shannon Penrod gives you important information and straight talk from one parent to another."

— Temple Grandin, Author of *The Way I See It*

"Shannon Penrod's story is about how one woman's trials as an autism mom created a context for her to become a transformative force for hope and love in her family and in autism families around the world. This book should be handed out to literally every parent whose child receives an autism diagnosis. Shannon's ability to be frank, vulnerable, compassionate, and hilarious at the same time is truly unique. You just aren't going to get a more truthful, hopeful, and meaningful message about being an autism parent anywhere else in the world. What's more, Shannon's message of values, hope, and hard work are universal messages that speak to human struggle. Not only will readers of this book learn how to be the most effective autism warrior parents they can be, they will connect with deep human meaning and purpose that will carry forward into all of life's struggles and triumphs."

— Dr. Jonathan Tarbox, PhD, BCBA-D Program Director, Master of Science in Applied Behavior Analysis, University of Southern California, and Director of Research, First Steps for Kids

"As parents of 3 Autistic citizens we only wish this incredibly insightful book had been available to us when our kids were first diagnosed. But we rejoice that it will help so many families. The chapter on insurance alone is worth the price of the book. Shannon Penrod's success is her ability to be relatable. To take her own story and let you be a part of it. She talks to you. Not at you. This book will be a lifesaver to parents that have a newly diagnosed child and to seasoned parents alike. I LOVED the 100 things to do with your child!"

— Navah Paskowitz-Asner & Matt Asner, Co-Founders of The Ed Asner Family Center

"Shannon has a way of taking the reader on her and her family's Autism Journey while making you laugh, cry, and also making you feel like you have earned a degree in all things Autism."

— Rachael Bird, Autism Advocate and Mother of Coby Bird

"Shannon Penrod teaches through vivid illuminating and empowering stories providing facts and antidotes gleaned as an Aut-Mom and One of America's top journalists on the Autism Beat."

— Vana Thiero, Emmy-Winning Journalist, Stand-Up Comic aka "V", and Filmmaker of *My Thiero Boys: A Lifestyle Dealing with Autism*

"A must read for anyone starting their autism journey and an excellent refresher for the well seasoned autism traveler. Shannon hit all the emotions with this book."

— Kerrie Mallory-Thompson, Autism Mom and Blogger of *Autism Will Not Define My Son*

"Shannon Penrod's book is the Autism Bible we all dreamed of having on the journey. It's funny, honest, raw and a guide, from what feels like, your very best friend. Each chapter an invaluable compass. A priceless must read for parents and professionals alike!"

— Jennifer St. Jude, Parent, Advocate, Social Worker, Adult on the Spectrum

AUTISM: PARENT TO PARENT

Sanity-Saving Advice for Every Parent with a Child on the Autism Spectrum

All marketing and publishing rights guaranteed to and reserved by:

FUTURE HORIZONS INC.

(817) 277-0727

(817) 277-2270 (fax)

E-mail: info@fhautism.com

www.fhautism.com

ISBN: 9781949177855

This book is dedicated to my husband, who gave me the two best gifts I have ever received: he loved me for who I am, not in spite of it, and he gave me our son. This book is also dedicated to my son and all of the wonderful people who make us parents in this unique club. Nobody ever thinks, "When I grow up, I hope I have a child on the Autism Spectrum!" but I wish I had, because it has been the greatest privilege of my lifetime to be my son's parent. Our children are the greatest teachers on the planet, and we are their humble students.

ACKNOWLEDGMENTS

I want to thank all the people who have been my teachers along the way. Dr. Sienna Greener Wooten, Sabrina Tooma, Peter Farag, Evelyn Kung, Soo Cho, Cecilia Knight, Jennifer Yakos, CJ Miyake, Art Wilke, Karen Nohelty, Veronica Hinojosa, Oscar Caballero, Katie DiRaimondo, Hank Moore, Vince Redmond, Dr. Evelyn Gould, Dr. Adel Najdowski, Dr. Jonathan Tarbox, Julie Kornack, Sara Litvak, Bryce Miler, Dr. Dennis Dixon, Joanne Lara, Matt Asner, Navah Paskowitz-Asner, Dr. Temple Grandin, Dr. Stephen Shore, Dr. Kerry Magro, Rachael Bird, Coby Bird, Jill Creter Harte, Spencer Harte, Joanne Allor, Kathy DeChellis, Karen Williams, Therese McLaughlin, Patty Penrod, Jerry and Jackie Miller, Nancy Alspaugh-Jackson, Emily Van Sickle, Samantha Leone, Travin Hardy, Lisa Ackerman, our fabulous Betsy, Kerrie Mallory-Thompson, Karen Delaney, Alex Plank, Vana Thiero, Kameena Ballard-Dawkins, Jennifer St. Jude, Holly Robinson Peete, Christine Stump, Christina Adams, Bonnie Yates, Jason Weissbrod, Garth Herberg, Craig and Natasha Duswalt, Mark Cole, Brian Williams, Oprah Winfrey, and a special thanks to the person without whom none of this would have been possible … Dr. Doreen Granpeesheh.

CONTENTS

FOREWORD

by Dr. Doreen Granpeesheh, Founder of the Center for Autism and Related Disorders, President of Autism Care Today!

Few people have meant as much to me as Shannon has. I am often astonished by her strength, her kindness, and her continued dedication to helping those whose lives have been affected by autism.

I first met Shannon in 2008. She had asked to interview me for her radio show. That morning, I had woken up very early, driven eighty miles to do a two-hour televised interview, and found myself exhausted by the time I sat in my car and awaited Shannon's call to answer questions on her radio show. Despite my somewhat unenergetic mood, within ten minutes of speaking with Shannon, I discovered a renewed sense of energy within myself. Her enthusiasm and positivity reminded me of the mission that had driven me forward for over twenty years. That first encounter was the beginning of a long and fruitful friendship—one that has brightened some of my darkest days and that continues to fuel my enthusiasm for remaining a positive force in the world of autism.

I entered the world of autism in 1978 as a student at UCLA, working with renowned psychologist Ivar Lovaas. I studied and worked with Lovaas for twelve years. During that time, we developed the framework for what is now called Applied Behavior Analysis, the most effective treatment modality for those affected by autism. In 1990, I founded the Center for Autism and Related Disorders (CARD) and, over the course of the following thirty years, grew CARD to 260 clinics, providing ABA therapy to thousands of individuals with autism around the world.

Shannon's son, Jem, who had been diagnosed with autism in 2006, was a patient at CARD. There were thousands of individuals receiving treatment at CARD, and I had the privilege of knowing only a few of them. Often, I would meet the children who had plateaued in their programs, and it was my job to problem-solve and modify our teaching techniques to help them re-engage and learn again. Sometimes, on rarer occasions, I had the great privilege of meeting children whose progress was so fast that we knew a removal of diagnosis was imminent. Jem was one such child, and when I met him, it was quite clear to me that he would have a bright and successful future. As I learned more about Jem and the progress he had made in treatment, I also learned about the struggles and hardships his parents had endured in order to get him there.

I had always been in awe of the parents. Even when I was a young student at UCLA, it was the parents and their dedication to their children that inspired me the most.

Shannon was one of the most inspiring parents I ever met. She shared with me all the fears parents experience when their child is diagnosed. She told me how our therapists had taught her to communicate differently with Jem, and most of all, she was a constant reminder that as parents, we go to any length to save our children.

As Jem flourished, Shannon's involvement in the world of autism increased. Her numerous contributions to families through her radio show and her presentations and as an eloquent speaker impressed me so much that I invited her to develop a web show. I promised to support her, as I knew other parents would benefit from hearing her story. That's when Shannon started Autism Live. She built a week-long series of shows, interviewing experts in the field and showcasing autism not only from the perspective of parents or providers, but also from the eyes of those on the spectrum themselves. She asked me if I would do a weekly show to answer the questions of parents who could not access professional help, and of course I wholeheartedly agreed. That was the inception of the Ask Dr. Doreen show, which is now in its eleventh year.

Through our weekly shows, Shannon and I developed a bond. We found great joy in helping others, and we became good friends. Every week, Shannon introduced me with kind and loving words, giving me great accolades as one of the most prominent experts in the field. But in truth, I was the one who learned from her. Hundreds of times, I watched Shannon go out of her way to help every family she encountered. I saw her spend countless hours researching issues for families, finding answers, calling people back at all times of the day and night, and even traveling long distances to bring comfort or advice to a family or to deliver food, toys, and other resources to those in need. Above all, I saw her remain dedicated, sincere, and loving toward every single person who reached out for help.

Shannon has a way of treating everyone as family. She is transparent, caring, dependable, and always willing to lend a helping hand. She shares everything she has, most valuable of which are her many years of experiences along the journey of autism. Having built her show into the number one autism podcast in the world, Shannon has been an incredible resource for those experiencing autism, either directly or through their loved ones. She has gained knowledge in a broad variety of areas pertaining to autism, including diets and nutrition, biological comorbidities, legal and funding issues, and of course ABA. Beyond that, Shannon has experienced firsthand the ups and downs families encounter as they search for answers.

In this book, Shannon shares with the reader lessons she learned on her quest. This is not a book of professional advice—there are many of those. This is a book written by a person who cares deeply about those on the spectrum of autism and their families. In this book, Shannon tells you all the things she wishes someone had told her when she was embarking on her journey—lessons that will undoubtedly lighten your load and give you direction as you maneuver through the maze of decisions you must make as a parent.

You may find books that tell you to start a diet for your child, but you will never find another book that tells you how to prepare for the lifelong changes that come with such a diet or how to mentally prepare for living a different life. Having listened to families who called into her shows for over ten years, Shannon knows exactly the questions that every family has, and without taking a side, she will tell you all the things to consider as you make your decisions.

There is no more valuable a gift than to have a guardian angel helping to guide you on your journey. This book is a valuable resource for all families living with autism. You will find great words of advice as well as guidance with difficult decisions. But most of all, this book will bring you comfort, a sense of peace and pride as you realize you are a member of the team that perseveres and, despite all odds, displays courage and joy at every turn of the journey of autism.

AUTHOR'S NOTE ON LANGUAGE

Words matter. They have the power to make us feel included or to divide us. It is only my intention to make everyone feel included in this book, but we do not all use the same words. I have chosen to identify myself as the "mom of an individual who was diagnosed as being on the Autism spectrum." Simply put, this is what my son is comfortable with, and I answer only to him on this subject. In this book I refer to "parents of individuals on the spectrum." To me, a "parent" is anyone who accepts the responsibility of looking after another's wellbeing. This is a commitment that transcends biology, time, and legal papers. Some of the best "parents" I have met would be legally defined as aunts, brothers, friends, grandparents, and other good people who cared and stood up for a child. In my book, they are all parents. You will also notice that I capitalize the word *Autism*. I understand that it is not grammatically correct, according to … someone. I choose to make my own rule on this. In my life, in my head, *Autism* warrants a capital "A." I apologize if this offends anyone; that is not my intent.

A NOTE TO
THE READER

This is a book for Parents who have children diagnosed with an Autism Spectrum Disorder, written by a Parent whose child was diagnosed with ASD. Let's be clear: I am not an expert in Autism. I am not a doctor, nor am I a person on the spectrum. I have great respect for experts, doctors, and adults on the spectrum. Their wisdom is invaluable, and I encourage you to read and listen to what they have to say on the subject. So why bother with me and what I have to say? I have a Parent merit badge after sixteen years of on-the-job training as a Mom of an individual with a diagnosis, three years 'experience hosting the radio program Everyday Autism Miracles, and more than ten years hosting *Autism Live*, the number one rated Autism podcast. I have interviewed thousands of experts, parents, and individuals on the spectrum, all in the hopes of helping myself and others be the best Parents we can be. If there were a PhD program in being a Parent of a person on the spectrum, I would be willing to sit for the equivalency exam. Still, I am well aware of the fact that there is a lot I don't know.

Here's what I do know: sometimes being a Parent, particularly to a child with ASD, can feel like the loneliest job on the planet. It isn't, but it sure feels that way. The irony is that there are millions of us all over the world feeling like we are the only ones going through it. I hope this book will remind you that you aren't alone, you aren't crazy, and better days are coming. I have tried to speak the truth, my truth, and sometimes that's a little too blunt for some. It is not my intention to offend anyone, ever...but sometimes it's necessary to say it like it is.

This book isn't intended to be read cover-to-cover, in order. Skim the chapter headings to see what jumps out at you. That's where you should begin. Then read chapters as you need them. You may be worlds past some of the chapters. Let those go. If you don't find what you need in the book, write to me at shannon@autism-live.com. I'm always happy to answer questions on Autism Live.

Spoiler Alert:

Being a parent of an individual on the Autism Spectrum can be very stressful, but I want to be clear that stress comes from all the things you have to do, all the fights you have to fight, hoops you have to jump through, ignorant people you have to put up with, financial craziness, and general BS you have to deal with PLUS the emotions you will have about all this, just to be able to feel you have done right by your child and given them every opportunity. Let's be clear: *the stress is not caused by our children.* Our children are beautiful. The stress is caused by everything but our children. If I can help you overcome any part of the stress or at least laugh at it so you can get back to the place where you can be with your child, then I will be happy that I have done my job.

Sincerely,

Shannon Penrod

Mom since 2003

CHAPTER
32

Other People's Opinion of My Parenting Is None of My Business

As a parent of an individual diagnosed with Autism, I have had the opportunity to practice many new skills on a daily basis. One of the greatest things I have learned is that "Other People's Opinion of My Parenting is None of My Business"—think about that for a moment. Read it back and then take a deep breath. This is the truth, and it is the road to forgiveness, sanity, and a happier place in the sun.

Notice that it doesn't say, "I'm sure no one's talking about me or my kid, or the way I feed/dress/discipline/raise/nurture/look at my child." Yeah…it doesn't say that, 'cause we all know that's not true. Everybody has an opinion! We can't change that, no matter what we do. In fact, there is no possibility that we could ever make everyone (*or even anyone*) happy with all of our parenting choices even if we devoted our every waking moment to it.

Stop and try to visualize what you would have to do to make the biggest current pain in your ass happy. I'm talking about the person whose voice you hear most often in your head. What would you have to do to make that person happy with your parenting? If you can, I want you to close your eyes for a second and picture everything you would have to do to make them happy. What would you have to give up to live the way this person thinks you should? What would you lose? And in the end, would they really be happy? Would you? Would your CHILD be happy? Is there any scenario in which you can picture your pain in the ass being happy while you are also happy and living the priorities that you hold closest? No? It's not *possible*, is it? Wow! Isn't it freeing to realize it can't be done?

It's not possible, so we can let it GO! Once we let it go, we get to do what we want to do, what makes sense, and what we have decided to do based on our needs, our kid's needs, and what we feel is right.

The great thing about this mindset is that is allows you to let go of the resentment of thinking, "They don't get it."

Truth Alert!

They don't get it! Nobody but you understands all that you have going on and all that you have to deal with. NOBODY!

Sure, other parents of individuals on the spectrum and other special needs parents have an understanding of what you are going through, but our kids are different, and our circumstances are different. Nobody but you knows what goes on in your house at 3 AM, so no one else's opinion is really valid anyway!

Anybody who is judging you is doing so with limited information...which, if you think about it, kind of makes them stupid. Honestly, if you said to me, "Do you think I should spend $300 on a dog?" The only sane response would be to say, "I don't know," and ask a bunch of questions: "Can you afford $300? Are you prepared to have the responsibility of having a dog? Are you allowed to have a dog where you live? Dogs live for a long time; are you prepared for the sacrifices and responsibilities that dog ownership brings?" I can think of hundreds of more questions that would be appropriate. Anything less than having those answers and I would have a truly uninformed opinion.

An uninformed opinion is what you are going to encounter over and over again as a parent in the world of Autism. Recognize it when you see it and school yourself to look the other way. You don't have to fix it. You are under no obligation to school the numbnut who offers their opinion as if it is the world's greatest gift when it is actually a turd in a punch bowl. It just isn't your business.

It has nothing to do with you and you aren't attached to it. It takes practice to get this mindset working.

Your mind will sometimes wonder if maybe they are right and you are wrong. Ask yourself this: This person giving advice, are they someone you would trust to leave your child with for a week, with no contact from you? If your answer is not an immediate yes, without reservations... then don't allow their opinion of you or your child another moment in your head. Sure, listen to advice and suggestions, but then freely weigh them on what you think and make the decision for yourself.

When it gets tough, say this, or something like this, to yourself...

Other people's opinion of my parenting is none of my business. I know what path I am on. I am making decisions based on what is good for my child today and in the long run. I am informed and involved in my child's growth and development. I take in information and I decide what is best for my child and for our family. I am strong and loving. I am a good parent.

Make it your mantra, sing it to a Disney theme song. Get it in your head, your heart, and your DNA. You've got this! Be proud! Other People's Opinion of my Parenting is none of my business!

CHAPTER

1

What's in a Diagnosis?

What is in a diagnosis? All right, let's get right down to the nitty-gritty. People will tell you all the time, "A diagnosis doesn't mean anything. Don't get emotional about it." Whenever someone says this, I always want to ask if they've ever had a child diagnosed with Autism Spectrum Disorder. Somehow the answer is always no, which makes me want to encourage them to keep their pie holes shut...but that would be rude and I don't want to appear rude. Sigh.

A diagnosis does matter. It's a beginning and an end. It comes with emotion because some things we thought were going to be may not ever be, and that feels like a death. Other things that we had not planned on are now a part of our reality, and that can feel overwhelming. There are questions and concerns. Can we afford this? Perhaps the scariest question, Can I do this?

When my son was diagnosed with Autism, I busily put on a brave face and told everyone it was going to be okay. I loudly and proudly announced that we were going to do everything we could for my son. No stone would be left unturned; we would find answers and get results! That's what I said...but I was shaking in my shoes. My guts felt like gelatin, and my head kept saying, "What if you can't do this? What if you just aren't up to this, Shannon? This sucks! Why did this happen to me?!" We'll talk more about this in the grief chapter, but suffice it to say that anything you feel is valid. The trick is to allow the feelings but keep taking action. Don't let your emotions paralyze you. Because your feelings will paralyze you if you don't really make an effort.

So, if getting a diagnosis feels like crap, we should all avoid it, right? No, just the opposite! Because guess what hurts worse than a diagnosis? NOT getting a diagnosis!

Ask any parent whose kid got a diagnosis years later what they would give to go back in time and get a diagnosis earlier. Or how about the poor parents who got a PDD NOS diagnosis? Which basically says "Yup, it's Autism, but not quite, not enough for us to give you help, come back when it's worse." Yeah, that's the seventh ring of hell. Ask those parents what it would have meant to have gotten a diagnosis earlier. They'll tell you: getting a diagnosis as early as possible is the best course of action. So if you don't have a diagnosis, and you think you qualify, run and rip that band-aid off.

Here are some good things that come with a diagnosis of Autism Spectrum Disorder:

1. *A prescription for treatment.* We don't know every-thing about Autism, but we know many ways of effectively helping individuals with Autism. It is essential that treatment be designed to meet the individual's unique needs, but some of the basics are getting the individual healthy and starting an early intensive behavioral intervention known as quality ABA or Applied Behavioral Analysis. Don't let ANYONE talk you out of it.

2. *FUNDING for treatment.* For many people, getting a diagnosis means getting funding for treatment. Treatment is expensive, so this is good. It doesn't mean it's easy. I have a theory that funding sources deliberately make it hard to apply for, get, and keep funding—so that everyone won't be willing to do the work to get it. Don't let them get away with that. Make it your part-time job to score all the funding you can, and celebrate loudly every time you get someone else to pay for what no one could possibly afford otherwise.

3. *Freedom from wondering.* For what it's worth, when you get the diagnosis, you get to move off the square where you wonder, "Oh, no, what if...?" You don't need to do that anymore. You know. Your kid has an Autism Spectrum diagnosis. You don't have to wonder; now you have to kick it into action.

What a diagnosis WON'T and CAN'T do:

1. *Predict the future.* Anyone who tells you what your child won't be able to do based on a diagnosis should be kicked with a pointed shoe. They are full of nasty chicken poo, and you can tell them I said so. So, no matter what you were told, remember that everybody's outcome is different, because everybody is different. With hard work and persistence, all individuals with Autism can and will make progress. Focus on doing the things that have been scientifically shown to be effective and shoot for the moon.

   Kids reveal themselves in miraculous ways. You won't be sorry. You will only be sorry if you don't. I can tell you endless stories of parents I have met who freely admit they didn't give their all to treatment when they had the opportunity. We can't judge these parents; for some of them it was the only decision they felt they could make. Don't judge them, but don't be like them. They live in the land of regret and what-ifs. Don't do that. Go all in right from the beginning and let your kids show you who they are.

2. *Explain Why.* To date we cannot definitively say what causes Autism. There is almost nothing that is certain except that both genetics and the environment

are involved. It is impossible to not ask, "Why?" All parents of children on the spectrum will eventually come to their own conclusions, or "hunches." You should be allowed that, but you will find that even within the Autism community there is no agreement, and often, unfortunately, no respect for what another parent believes. I will only tell you that if you are deciding to have another child and would like to reduce the risk of having another child with ASD, you should look very closely at the work of Dr. David Berger and his study on reducing autism risks in pregnant women.[1]

Who Can Give a Diagnosis of Autism Spectrum Disorder (ASD)?

Generally, a diagnosis of ASD comes from either a developmental pediatrician or a trained, licensed psychologist. Often your insurance will cover all or a significant portion of the cost of an assessment, but check before you schedule the appointment; the fees can be staggering. Sometimes people will pay to get a diagnosis from a source that is not tied to their funding. I think we can all recognize that getting a truly impartial opinion would be the best possible choice, but the cost is often too high for it to be considered. My advice is usually to get the diagnosis through your

1. http://forump2i.com/wp-content/uploads/2018/10/P2i-CS-02.26.18.pdf

insurance. If you don't feel like the diagnosis is accurate or thorough, then get a second opinion.

The actual diagnosis:

There is a lot of confusion around a diagnosis, mainly because the criteria for diagnosis changes periodically. At the time of writing this book, we use the DSM-V. I have provided a link to it at the end of this chapter. Feel free to read it thoroughly, but here's what I think is essential for a parent to know:

1. There are two numbers given with the diagnosis. They rate severity in two categories: Social Communication and Restricted and Repetitive Behaviors. A 3 rating means that the individual requires very substantial support in that area. A 2 rating means they need substantial support in that area, and a 1 rating means they require support in that area. Don't get stuck in the numbers. The numbers can and do change with treatment. Obviously, the goal is for someone to need as little support as possible, but this only happens if the right amount of support is given. So if your child has 3s or 2s, feel the grief of that, but get busy. The scary thing I see is kids with 1s whose parents are told, "It's mild. I wouldn't bother with intensive treatment." Sometimes this advice comes from a well-meaning but basically ignorant pediatrician. Be careful. It

is the rare pediatrician who knows about effective treatment for Autism. If your child has a diagnosis of ASD with a severity rating of 1,1, by definition it means THEY NEED SUPPORT. Make sure they get it, and let no one talk you out of it. Believe me, people will try to talk you out of it. To me this is beyond stupid; it would be like saying: your child definitely needs glasses, the test shows they need glasses—but let's not bother with them. He'll be able to see what he can see, and that will work out fine. Maybe he'll outgrow it. Stupidity! Don't get sucked into it. A 1 means "needs support, get support." Simple.

2. There are qualifiers that may come with the diagnosis. These are additional diagnoses a person qualifies for that are separate from Autism but that will have an impact on the Autism and its treatment.

For example: a child may be diagnosed with Autism Spectrum Disorder with intellectual disability and be given a severity rating of 3,3.

Another child may be diagnosed with Autism Spectrum Disorder with ADHD and a 1,2 rating.

All of this is very emotion provoking. It can be devastating to sit and hear this being said about your child. It's important to remember to breathe and to remember why you are subjecting yourself and your child to this: because this is the way you get help. Keep your head tuned there, and say this or something like this:

My child is exactly who they were yesterday. A diagnosis doesn't change that, but my child needs help and support. I am going to keep breathing so I can get them the support they need. All this diagnosis means is my child is eligible for help. It doesn't change who they are. I am breathing and advocating for my child. It's going to be okay.

Once you get a diagnosis, you may be referred to someone else for further evaluation or for treatment recommendations. At some point a prescription will be written for the amount of therapy your child needs. *This is the big deal.* This is where you need to pay attention. This is where people get screwed in the drive thru all the time. Don't be afraid to ask questions. Our current medical climate doesn't support asking questions, but do it anyway. I have had a doctor tell me that I was asking too many questions. You know what I did? I asked a bunch more questions: "Since when is asking a question a bad thing? Are my questions making you nervous? Why do you think it bothers you that I'm asking so many questions?" Boy, that one stopped her. She looked at me and she said honestly, "We are given quotas we have to fill, which means we are only allowed a certain amount of time with each patient. Your questions are making me get behind." But as soon as she said it, it made her stop. She sat down and said,

"You're right. You should be able to ask as many questions as you want." Yeah, that's the truth! So ASK.

Ask: Who is going to be writing the treatment prescription?

Ask: What are they going to write the prescription for? When they say the amount, if it is less than forty hours, ask why. There are lots of reasons why but very few that you should accept.

Below I have a list of "reasons" and quippy comebacks to shut them down. The discussion I have given is based on having a child who is under the age of five and who has not yet started kindergarten. At that point you should be fighting for forty hours a week. I know. It sounds crazy! Forty hours a week for a three-year-old? That's a full-time job!!! Please hear me say to you that I too thought it was crazy. Then I read the studies, and I started to fight for forty hours! If you have a child who is already in school and is older, you can still ask for forty hours, but it is an uphill climb. If you decide not to, fight for at least thirty, and don't ever settle for less than twenty-five hours of therapy a week.

I suggest that you make your stand in the office with the person writing the prescription. If you leave and try to take the argument to your insurance provider, it is going to be long, arduous, and messy. Eventually it is going to end up with you either paying for a second opinion or going back to the office to have this discussion with the prescription writer another day. Save time. Be prepared. Be nice but immovable. Get the prescription right on day 1.

Doctor says:
Your child is too young for forty hours a week.

You say:
I have studies that show that forty hours a week is what is effective; we'll have to ramp up to that, but I don't want to have to come back in a month to get the right prescription.

Doctor says:
Your child is too old for forty hours a week.

You say:
I have studies that show that older kids need intensive hours to catch up. We'll make it work. Please don't give up on my child because he/she didn't get the diagnosis early enough.

Doctor says:
Your child is very high-functioning; they don't need forty hours a week.

You say:
Actually, I have studies that show that the high-functioning kids are the ones who respond the best to intensive behavioral intervention at forty-plus hours a week. We are

committed to *helping* our child have the best possible out-come. Please don't shortchange my child.

Doctor says:
ABA isn't really effective for all kids. It's really hard on them. I don't think you should put him/her through that many hours.

You say:
Thank you, but we have done our research and we have seen that kids who get forty hours make significantly more progress. That's what has been shown to be effective, and that is what we are committed to do for our child.

Doctor says:
Let's start with twenty hours a week and see how they do.

You say:
Thank you, but I've done my research, and twenty hours hasn't been shown to be effective in creating the highest level of progress. That would be like giving me half a pre-scription for an antibiotic. We both know I would be back needing the full prescription. I would like the full prescrip-tion for ABA treatment. Forty hours, please.

Doctor says:
We just don't write prescriptions for forty hours.

You say:
    I can show you over 100 studies that show more hours

is what is effective. Can you show me ONE that shows that twenty hours is effective? (Spoiler alert: there aren't any studies showing that twenty hours is as effective as forty.)

Be firm. Be polite. Be immovable. Get the prescription. It is what will be the biggest determining factor in your child's outcome.

Say this or something like this to yourself:

I am going to get and give my child their full prescription, because that is what science says works. I will not be deterred from giving my child what is considered the proper amount of therapy in their individual case. I going to give my child, myself, and my family this opportunity to make the maximum progress.

Resources

DSM V Diagnostic Criteria: https://www.cdc.gov/ncbddd/autism/hcp-dsm.html

Studies showing intensity of ABA therapy is effective:

Cohen, Howard, Mila Amerine-Dickens, and Tristram Smith. "Early Intensive Behavioral Treatment." *Journal of Developmental & Behavioral Pediatrics* 27, no. Supplement 2 (April 27, 2006). https://doi.org/10.1097/00004703-200604002-00013.

Eikeseth, Svein, Tristram Smith, Erik Jahr, and Sigmund Eldevik. "Intensive Behavioral Treatment at School for 4- to 7-Year-Old Children with Autism." *Behavior Modification*

26, no. 1 (January 26, 2002): 49–68. https://doi.org/10.11 77/0145445502026001004.

Eldevik, Sigmund, Richard P. Hastings, J. Carl Hughes, Erik Jahr, Svein Eikeseth, and Scott Cross. "Meta-Analysis of Early Intensive Behavioral Intervention for Children with Autism." *Journal of Clinical Child & Adolescent Psychology* 38, no. 3 (2009): 439–50. https://doi. org/10.1080/15374410902851739.

Linstead, Erik, Dennis R. Dixon, Ryan French, Doreen Granpeesheh, Hilary Adams, Rene German, Alva Powell, Elizabeth Stevens, Jonathan Tarbox, and Julie Kornack. "Intensity and Learning Outcomes in the Treatment of Children with Autism Spectrum Disorder." *Behavior Modification* 41, no. 2 (2016): 229–52. https://doi. org/10.1177/0145445516667059.

Sallows, Glen O., and Tamlynn D. Graupner. "Intensive Behavioral Treatment for Children with Autism: Four-Year Outcome and Predictors." *American Journal on Mental Retardation* 110, no. 6 (November 2005): 417–38. https:// doi.org/10.1352/08958017.

CHAPTER
2
My To-Do List

Lisa Ackerman, the founder of The Autism Community in Action (TACA), is fond of saying, "When your child is diagnosed with Autism, it's not 'Game Over'; it's 'Game On.'"

Dr. Jonathan Tarbox encourages parents to think of early intervention like you would think of getting a gifted child ready for the Olympics. There would be an extended period of time where sacrifices would need to be made in order for this extraordinary training to happen, but it wouldn't be forever, and it would be worth it in the end.

I like to warn people that if you do Early Intensive Behavioral Intervention right—and you SHOULD—it will feel like someone picked up your life, shook it, and set it back down on its side. So how do you prepare for that?

1. *Get yourself healthy, get everyone else in the family healthy, and make health, mental and physical, a priority.* Can I just admit that I didn't do this and it is my biggest regret? Autism is a marathon, not a sprint. If you don't prioritize health, someone is going to get sick, and everything you have worked for will

be in jeopardy. We all know this intellectually, but many of us, me included, will prioritize our children's health and treatment and put our own on a back burner. Bad idea. First, your kid needs you, which means you have to be healthy and alive. Second, you need to model the behavior of self-care for your child. Your child needs to see a daily example of what it looks like to take care of one's own health. Set a good example, take care of yourself. Live to see all the good things your child will do. Don't make me tell you the horror stories of parents who neglected their own health and died; don't...don't make me do it. Prioritize health. Get on it today.

2. *Clear the decks.* Is there stuff that you were just barely dealing with before but you're sick to your stomach thinking how you're going to manage now? Time to cut some ties. You are about to become the project manager for one of the biggest jobs you will ever do in your life, so you may not be able to run the PTA bake sale this year, or go for that promotion, or deal with Aunt Sally's chemo, or write that script you've been working on. For now. You can come back to it later, if you choose to. Right now, you need to get focused, and that may mean saying goodbye to people, projects, and even potentially jobs that suck all your time and energy. A word to the wise,

though: don't get rid of the job that keeps the roof over your head and the food on the table until you have something else that will replace it. And whatever you do, don't start your own business right now! Yep, I made that mistake too.

3. *Circle the wagons.* You are going to need some help. Make peace with that and get over it. Pushy, I know—but I'm not going to coddle you on this one. We all like to think that we should be able to "do it on our own"—but we can't, and who really wants to? Think of it this way: it feels good to help other people, doesn't it? Why are you denying people the pleasure of helping you so they can feel better? Yes, there are some people who are going to hurt your feelings by not showing up for you. Somebody is going to let you down by not being there for you. Just remember that has more to do with them than it has to do with you. Some people don't deal well with challenges. It's shocking. Even disappointing. But it is never a sign that you weren't worthy, just that they weren't up to it. You will find plenty of people who will surprise you with how helpful they are. Forgive the people who aren't helpful and enjoy discovering the people in your life who are helpful. Lean into them, thank them! You won't make it without them.

4. *Prioritize quality ABA in the full prescription.* This is so important, I'm going to say it again... Prioritize quality ABA in the full prescription. Hopefully you have a prescription for ABA therapy; if not, ask for one. Read Chapter 1 for help with this. In today's environment, with insurance paying for ABA in all states in the US, it is very common to have a prescription for ABA but at too few hours. Between the ages of three and five, the only appropriate prescription is for thirty to forty hours week. It is more likely to see prescriptions for ten to twenty hours a week. There are no studies showing that ten to twenty hours of ABA is effective. There is one clear study showing that ten hours a week is NOT effective. There are hundreds of studies that show that thirty to forty hours a week is effective. I have referenced a handful of them at the end of Chapter 1. If you have a prescription for a lower amount, you will need to contact your insurance company, reference the studies, and ask for an appeal. They will relent, but it may take time. Often this doesn't happen until the second appeal. Be a squeaky, informed wheel. Let them know you are one of "those parents" who isn't going to drop it. They don't have a leg to stand on, so don't give up. Then when you have the hours, you need to use them. It's going to be hard. Your

provider isn't going to have enough behavior technicians; help them to hire more people. I'm serious. Recommend your friend's college-aged kids, recruit people while you are in line at Starbucks, get solution-minded, and don't let anything stop you from getting that full prescription. Don't cancel therapy sessions for anything short of illness. This sounds easy. It's not. My best friend had cancer when my kid was in his first year of therapy. This was back in the day when the parent had to be there for the ABA session. My friend asked me to take her to chemo. I said no, my son and I went to therapy. It was hard. Someone else had to take her. There are people who won't agree with me, but this isn't their book and they didn't have to live through what I did, so their opinion is none of my business (see Chapter 32). I prioritized my kid's treatment over everything, and I can tell you that I will never be sorry about that. If you make it your priority, you won't be sorry either.

5. *Write a Manifesto!* Life is often hard and confusing. Then you get tired, and it gets even harder to make decisions. Having a clear statement of purpose makes it easier. In my family we called that statement of purpose our "Manifesto." We took a blank piece of paper, and we wrote down what was most important to us. We deliberately kept the list short

in our son's first year of therapy. We put our son's therapy first. My husband's career was on the list. Mine was not that first year. My choice, I cleared my decks, not sorry, my career is fine. Staying together as a family was on the list. Making a million dollars—not on the list. Buying a house—not on the list. Stuff came up. It got confusing. I was offered a job. It wasn't what was best for my son's therapy. A house came along. It wasn't going to work. Not with the priorities on the list. Over the years, the manifesto changed as our family's needs and goals changed. I can tell you this: the things on the list flourished under the attention we gave them. If you truly want to accomplish something, put it on the list. I recommend putting your child's therapy at the top of the list for at least two years, potentially longer. Worth it... So, so, so very worth it.

My life is filled with moments where I will be doing something, anything, real-life moments, laundry, shopping, watching TV, whatever, but I'll be interacting with my son and he will say something, something honest, insightful, funny—often very witty, and it will show me who he is, who he is growing to be, what he is thinking, and how he sees the world, and in those moments I am often stunned into silence because I am so very grateful for all I have. This is why I urge you to make your child's therapy a priority. It is worth it.

6. *Practice Mindfulness.* Take at least a couple of minutes a day to breathe and allow yourself to be. You may have to do this in the car, after you have strapped everyone into their car seats but before you put the car in drive. This journey you are on is a marathon, not a sprint. Do whatever you can to stay centered. There are apps, and the internet is filled with free meditations. Even a small amount of mindfulness has been shown to be effective at helping parents with stress, and guess what? Those parents were shown to be more effective in helping their kids. There is a growing community of people practicing ACT (Acceptance Commitment Therapy) with parents of individuals with ASD. I can personally recommend it. It simply gives you tools to deal with the feelings you have. It never asks you to deny those feelings or to "Suck it up." I don't know about you; I'm no good at sucking it up. Allowing myself to have my feelings, getting clear about what they are, and giving them a context is what helps me. The perfect example of this was when my son was ten. After his intensive ABA, he was doing better, and he wanted to do all of the things a ten-year-old does: walk down the street to a friend's house by

himself, go into a public restroom by himself, cross the street by himself. Now, if you asked me what was most important in my life at that time, I would have told you "Helping my son to be independent!" but I wasn't letting him do all the independent things because I was SCARED! So I would just say no! People kept telling me to get over my fear! HA!!! Like that's possible! Just get over it! Yeah, right! ACT taught me to acknowledge my fears and where they sprang from. It taught me to acknowledge my competing priorities. It hadn't even occurred to me that I could keep my kid safe AND teach him to be independent. In fact, teaching him good independence skills was the way to keep him safe! I was able to see that these things could be in opposition, or they could work together. We made a plan for a safe transition to him doing all the things he wanted to do and the things that would prepare him to be safe and independent. I encourage everyone to look at ACT.

7. *Celebrate.* Everything. Any chance you get. This might sound ridiculous, but this is some of the best advice I can give you. There are going to be small victories... celebrate them. There are going to be huge moments of triumph... celebrate them. I don't want to candy coat it; you are in for some

bumpy stuff, but if you are willing to celebrate ALL the victories, you will come to see that this journey has some truly great moments. It's going to be really meaningful to you when your child is able to communicate with you. Celebrate the hey-nonny-nonny out of it. Yes, you have friends whose kids just talked like it was no big deal—but you know what? It came to them so easily that they didn't jump up and down and celebrate it like it was major miracle. You get to. Take advantage of it! Dance in the living room! Howl at the moon! It will help remind you of the amazing path you are on. You are rocking it and showing up for your amazing kid. Celebrate it and celebrate them!

Say this or something like this to yourself:

My family is going to do something amazing. We are going to work together for a period of time to help a very important member of our family be all they can be. We are prioritizing our health and our well-being so we can all be our best and give this period of time everything we've got. We will not live with regret wondering what we could have done. We will take each day as it comes. We will forgive ourselves for not always being perfect, but we will celebrate every victory, large or small. We will look back on this time with pride and know that we truly did something amazing ... together.

Resources

Harris, Russ. *Reality Slap: How to Survive and Thrive When Life Hits Hard.* London: Robinson, 2021. (A great book on Acceptance Commitment Therapy, by a parent of a child with ASD.)

CHAPTER

3

Diet

Number one on your to-do list was to get everybody healthy, so let's take a minute to talk about diet. There are a lot of Autism diets. A lot. Eventually, you are going to want to know more about them because chances are you, your child on the spectrum, and maybe even someone else in your household can benefit from one of more of them—but I think it's best to start easy, so let's start with getting your diet clean. What does that mean?

1. Reduce pesticides and chemicals in your food.
2. Reduce processed and artificial foods in your diet.

I never used to pay much attention to the organic thing until a study came out in May of 2011 showing that the amount of pesticide in a child's urine coincided with their amount of "hyperactivity" symptoms.[2] This made no sense to me, so I started asking questions.

I started with the word "pesticide"—which seems to pair "pest" and the suffix "cide," which means to kill—kill

2. Xu, X., W. N. Nembhard, H. Kan, G. Kearney, Z.-J. Zhang, and E. O. Talbott. "Urinary Trichlorophenol Levels and Increased Risk of Attention Deficit Hyperactivity Disorder among US School-Aged Children." *Occupational and Environmental Medicine* 68, no. 8 (2011): 557–61. https://doi.org/10.1136/oem.2010.063859.

them bugs! But how does a pesticide kill a bug? Hold on to your seat cushions, because the ride is about to get bumpy!

Modern-Day Pesticides Are Neurotransmitter Toxins.

Neurotransmitter toxins affect how the brain of the pest interacts with its extremities. Generally, given in proper amounts, pesticides make the bug's legs so restless that they lose focus and consequently forget to eat. They die eventually from starvation.

WHAT?

And when pesticide is given in larger doses, the pest's legs move *so much* that the pathway is overstimulated to the point that it shuts down and paralysis occurs. The bug is frozen, can't eat, and eventually dies from starvation.

Okay. That's what it does to bugs, so what does it do to humans? More and more studies are showing a correlation to the amount of pesticide in our systems and hyperactivity or lack of focus... Sound familiar?

More and more experts are recommending that we all lower the pesticides and chemicals in our food. It is more expensive, but I suggest going on a mindfully organic diet for thirty days. See if you feel a difference and if you see a difference in your kids. I think you will decide it's worth it.

I also recommend checking the "Clean 15 and the Dirty Dozen" list[3] on a yearly basis to find out which fruits and vegetables are the most necessary to buy organic (hint: never eat a pepper if it's not organic). With the list you can save money and time.

I think your family will also notice that organic tastes better. Don't tell them you've changed anything, and let them tell you if they notice a difference. My husband is the biggest skeptic in the world, and even he'll tell you that nothing is better than organic orange juice and that it's not even in the same family with non-organic orange juice. Don't get him started on pudding made with organic milk! He'll tell you it's a spiritual experience and not to be missed.

Once you've gone organic, it's time to reduce sugar and artificial colors. Not sure? Go to a kid's birthday party and watch the kids all playing and running and laughing. Watch them serve the cake with the colorful, sweet icing and take a peek at your watch. Check on those same happy kids ten to twenty minutes later... What you will see is kids crying, squabbling, and throwing tantrums, and moms quickly packing them up, apologizing, saying they must be tired from all the playing... except the three kids who didn't happen to have cake seem to be just

3. LaMotte, Sandee. "Dirty Dozen 2021: View the List of Foods with the Most and Least Pesticides." CNN. Cable News Network, March 17, 2021. https://www.cnn.com/2021/03/17/health/dirty-dozen-foods-2021-wellness/index.html.

fine. Hmmm ... What's that about? Artificial colors are evil, and they do evil things to kids. Children with Autism don't need extra stuff to mess them up. Get rid of it, all of it, and start reading labels. You will be shocked where they are putting artificial colors these days.

What about sugar? Sugar isn't evil, but we consume so much more of it than is healthy. An added concern, many of our kids with Autism have Candida issues, an over-growth of yeast. Regular sugar consumption will make it hard for those kids to ever concentrate. Best to minimize sugar as much as possible.

Once you are organic, with no artificial colors and low/no sugar, it's time to look at the main taproot of all Autism Diets: the gluten-free/casein-free diet. This is the diet that almost everyone should try for at least six months to see if their child is helped. It is true that not everyone bene-fits from this diet, but many of us have seen significant improvement in our kids as a result, so I urge you to try it. No gluten (a protein found in grain), no casein (a protein found in milk) ... none ... This is not a diet about reducing; it's about elimination. At first it is normal to think this is impossible! Don't most children live on chicken strips and mac and cheese? Don't despair. There is so much support for a GFCF diet on the internet, including recipes and sam-ple menus, that it is easier than ever to implement. There are even great chicken strips and mac and no cheese that you can buy at most grocery stores now. And some of them are actually better than their gluten-filled cousins. When family was visiting, I fed their kids the organic gluten-free chicken strips we get at our grocery store. Weeks later, the mom called me and asked for the brand because her kids were asking for the ones they had had at my house. Sometimes gluten free is better-tasting. This is not always the case; you will run into stuff that has less flavor than cardboard and the consistency of sand. It's out there too. Ask people on the diet for suggestions or tune in to Autism Live; we have a whole playlist of tasty recipes. Life is too short to eat bad-tasting food, and you don't have to do so in order to be GFCF.

I will just say that my child lost all of his verbal language and didn't begin to speak again until he was on the GFCF diet. In my opinion, it's worth trying. But the asterisk is that you must completely eliminate gluten and casein and stay that way for at least six months to see if there is a difference. Even minor infractions can mess a child up for weeks.

My son was once given pretzels without my knowledge at a gym daycare. He was like a wild animal when I picked him up, and I had no idea what was wrong. I remember crying to my husband because we hadn't seen that kind of behavior since we had started the diet and I had thought the diet had eliminated this behavior. I was sure there hadn't been an infraction, so in my mind the diet couldn't have fixed it. Fortunately, one of the workers at the gym confided in me and told me they had seen the director of the daycare feed my son some pretzels, which were full of gluten and dairy. I was mad but relieved. It was clear proof that the diet was working and that his wild, extreme behaviors were being caused by gluten and dairy. In case you're wondering if I complained to the gym, I did. They informed us they couldn't handle a child with Autism and that our son was no longer welcome— but that's a whole other *Oprah*. We lost a gym, but I have never regretted it. In a weird way, it made me fully appreciate the importance of the diet and of not allowing any infractions.

Do yourself a favor and try the GFCF diet, then you can branch out into other diets to see what works best for you.

A Word of Caution

There are more and more foods available in mainstream stores and restaurants that are labeled gluten-free/dairy-free. Use caution; many of these foods are loaded with artificial colors and flavors. Some of these foods are processed in plants that also process wheat and dairy. You will need to decide for yourself how careful you are going to be.

You may want to consider getting your child tested for allergies. If you do this, consider asking for a full IgE/IgA/IgG panel and getting to see the full results. This is not allergy testing like it used to be. Nobody gets scratched, but blood is drawn. You will be able to see not only what your child is currently reacting to, but also what they are becoming allergic to and what foods you should be cautious about giving them.

I am someone who has suffered from food allergies my whole life. It is an emotional roller coaster. You just feel horrible when you've had something you are reactive to. It's miserable and it's hard to focus on anything else. Take food allergies/sensitivities seriously. I get really ticked off when people say food and diet have nothing to do with Autism. Excuse me! Individuals with ASD are people, and people react to what they put in their bodies. If I am preparing for a physics test and I eat a bunch of sugar and drink alcohol the night before, I might not perform as well on the test. Athletes are very careful about what they eat before big games. Why? Because what they put in their bodies affects their performance. Now, I can eat what an Olympic athlete eats, but it is not going to make me a world-class athlete, right? However, it will affect my performance. Changing your child's diet is not going to miraculously change their Autism Spectrum Diagnosis, but it may change their performance as you try to get them caught up on what they haven't learned.

Say this, or something like this to yourself:

What we put into our bodies matters. I am prioritizing putting healthy food into my family's bodies so we can be our best selves. Every individual is different, and what my family needs may be different than what others eat. We are worth the time and effort it takes to eat what is right for us.

Resources

Silberberg, Barrie. *The Autism & ADHD Diet: A Step-by-Step Guide to Hope and Healing by Living Gluten Free and Casein Free (GFCF) and Other Interventions.* Sourcebooks, 2009.

Matthews, Julie. *Nourishing Hope: Nutrition and Diet Guide for Healing Children.* Self-published, Healthful Living Media, 2007.

Lewis, Lisa S. *Special Diets for Special Kids.* Future Horizons, Inc., 2011.

Seroussi, Karyn, and Lisa S. Lewis. *The Encyclopedia of Dietary Interventions for the Treatment of Autism and Related Disorders: The Essential Reference Guide for Parents and Physicians.* Sarpsborg Press, 2008.

Seroussi, Karyn. *Unraveling the Mystery of Autism and Pervasive Developmental Disorder: A Mother's Story of Research and Recovery.* Broadway Books, 2002.

LaMotte, Sandee. "Dirty Dozen 2021: View the List of Foods with the Most and Least Pesticides." CNN. Cable News Network, March 17, 2021, https://www.cnn.com/2021/03/17/health/dirty-dozen-foods-2021-wellness/index.html.

"Family Resources." The Autism Community in Action (TACA), May 28, 2021, https://tacanow.org/family-resources/.

"Autism Live." Autism Live, http://www.autism-live.com/. (What's Left playlist features recipes for Gluten-Free, Dairy-Free eaters.)

CHAPTER 4

ABA

What can I say? You need good ABA. A lot of people are going to tell you that you don't need ABA or that you shouldn't waste too much time on it. None of them will be parents of kids who are doing very well. I suggest you think about that and talk to parents of kids who are doing great. They will tell you. I will tell you. Make this your immovable thing and rotate everything else around it for at least two years, maybe more. You won't be sorry. Act like it's life and death. It might be.

Truth Alert

All ABA (Applied Behavior Analysis) is not the same. There is some unbelievably BAD ABA out there; you definitely do not want that. I am encouraging you to get excellent-quality ABA that takes the individual learner into consideration, including their SENSORY NEEDS. In a later chapter, you will hear me encourage you to listen to self-advocates and their harrowing stories of ABA that did NOT take into consideration their unique sensory needs. We must listen to these stories and respect them. We must not allow what happened to these people to be repeated. We must not allow our children to be traumatized in this way. I know it gets scary here. None of us wants our children to be traumatized. Many people are so scared by the prospect that they will say no to ABA. Instead, as a mother who watched excellent-quality ABA help her son to learn all that he needed to learn, I want to help you be watchdogs looking for good ABA and refusing anything that does not adhere to exacting standards of individualized, trauma-informed, compassionate care. Good ABA is out there, and those of us who have had the benefit of it want to help you find it. However, I also want to acknowledge that even though I believe strongly that everyone should try good-quality ABA, you may find that it isn't the right fit for you, your family, or your child. There are other therapies. There are other methods. You will find they have less research and are thus harder to fund with insurance, but that is also changing. If you live in the United States, chances are your child is eligible for ABA funding;. It can be a game-changer; it was for my family, so let's give you some guidelines to help you recognize if you are getting the good stuff.

Hallmarks of Quality ABA

1. *Quality ABA is individualized to the child's needs.* This means the therapy has to take into account the

individual's learning styles, what they like, what they don't like, and their SENSORY NEEDS and TRIGGERS. It also has to consider if this child/teen/adult has experienced trauma or if there are things that would potentially be traumatic for them. If you truly want to teach someone, traumatizing them is never the way.

2. *Quality ABA incorporates parents, caregivers, and family members.* Everybody needs to learn this! You can't just drop the kids off, pick them up later, and hope it's all working out. You have to learn it and use it. Once you understand it and see how it works, you will want to use it. Your parenting life will improve exponentially.

3. *Quality ABA plans for generalization from the beginning.* This means they are going to teach the child many different ways to do something so that in the real world, they will be able to learn new ways on their own. For example: Lots of kids are toilet-trained but only want to pee in the toilet at home. This is because someone didn't properly plan for generalization: first you teach on the potty at home, then you have them pee at Starbucks, then at Target, etc. You are never going to be able to teach all toilets in the world, that would be crazy, but if you plan properly and visit lots of different toilets, the child will eventually get it—this is what peeing is, no matter where. Voila! We have generalization! Every single lesson your child has should have a

plan for generalization from the very first lesson, or it's not good-quality ABA!

4. *Quality ABA NEVER blames the child if they are not learning.* Quality ABA changes the teaching technique if learning isn't happening. Think about that. The child isn't wrong; the teaching method isn't working. Change the teaching method and the child will learn! By the way, science has proven ABA (quality ABA) is the most effective teaching strategy.

5. *Quality ABA never uses aversives in treatment.* You will hear endless stories of ABA people using horrible aversive strategies, electric shock, hot sauce, spraying with water, etc. during ABA sessions with children with Autism. This is not true and would be unethical. So where do these rumors come from? In the early years of behavior modification for Autism—before it was called ABA therapy—people tried using aversives to see if it would change a child's behavior. These methods were found to be ineffective and cruel. They are no longer used, and if your ABA provider is using them, you need a new ABA provider. The Judge Rottenberg Center is an example of a place that still uses aversives. Don't take your child to any place that uses aversives.

6. *Is the child making progress on things that are meaningful to THEIR life? Is the child learning to communicate?* This

might be functional communication or vocal speech; all communication styles are valid. I love Dr. Temple Grandin's guidance on this. She says, "When I talk to parents of very young, two- to five-year-old children, I always ask if their child is making progress. Some of the signs of effective teaching and progress are more speech, learning how to wait and take turns at games, and learning skills such as dressing. The child should always like going to therapy. If the child hates therapy, the therapist may be forcing them into sensory overload. These signs of progress for a young child are the same regardless of the name of the therapy."

7. *The Test.* Are they learning how to get their needs met or are they only learning how to comply? It is vital that this be considered. My very favorite quote from Dr. Granpeesheh is "It has to be fair." If a child is being asked to do something, we need to consider what is in it for them. Learning needs to be fun and fair. If the child is not making progress on things that are meaningful to them, either because they have stagnated and are just doing the same thing over and over OR their day is filled with lessons that have no clear benefit for them and that only seek to have them "fit in"... then this is not good ABA; look for another program. Good ABA is not about "fitting in" or changing someone to fit someone else's idea of normal—that is

the bad ABA. Good ABA teaches skills that help individuals to leap hurdles. This is what I want you to find. I did.

Manipulation Alert

People will tell you...

1. ABA isn't effective for kids who are high-functioning!

LIE!

Quality ABA is extremely effective at helping kids who are high-functioning!

2. ABA isn't effective for kids who are profoundly affected by Autism.

LIE!

Quality ABA can help those individuals with functional communication skills to enrich their lives and the lives of those who care for them!

3. ABA will turn your child into a robot!

LIE!

Good quality ABA creates unique, happy, polite children who understand rules but are creative, have senses of humor, and are deeply imaginative. They also understand how to have boundaries and how to communicate their own desires.

4. Forty hours of therapy is too much for a little kid; twenty is more reasonable!

LIE!

Studies have shown conclusively that forty hours of therapy is what is effective. If your doctor prescribed an antibiotic for you, would you take half of it and expect to have a good result? NO! There are NO studies showing that twenty hours of therapy is effective, but hundreds showing that forty is. Follow the science.

5. ABA isn't effective for teenagers!

LIE!

ABA is a teaching tool that is effective with people of all ages. Quality ABA that focuses on an individualized program, often with Social Skills, Cognition, and Executive Functions lessons is VERY effective at helping teens on the spectrum.

6. ABA isn't for everyone.

LIE!

Everyone, everyone is capable of making progress using ABA techniques. The principles of ABA are used in business to train Olympic athletes and in all settings where teaching needs to be effective.

So if ABA is so great, why are people telling so many lies about it?

TRUTH ALERT

ABA is very expensive.

You're familiar with the Grand Canyon, right? Deep, big...created by water drops, over and over, time, water, time, water, deep, big. ABA is similar in that it takes time. Over and over, time. Paying a patient, trained person, time. Forty hours a week. $$$. The first year my son had therapy, I think we determined the bill was around $120,000. Don't look at me! I didn't pay it; I couldn't afford that! Back then the good old state of California paid for it. California understood that they could pay out roughly $350,000 to help my son early in his life and the result would likely be that he would live independently and have a job that allowed him to pay taxes the rest of his life OR they could say tough toenails to the therapy bill and chances are my son would have required support his whole life to the tune of roughly $2.4 million. California understood this equation and rightly made an investment in my child. Don't talk bad about California to me; it makes me crabby.

Now, it is usually insurance that pays for ABA therapy. Insurance doesn't like to pay for things, and they have a long-standing history of making it hard for people to get expensive services. If they move slowly in their approvals, it saves them money. If they spend a little less here and approve a little less there...it saves them money. If every parent of an individual with ASD stood up and said, "My kid is getting forty hours no matter what crap you throw at me," insurance would have a total meltdown. Especially because a lot of kids would get a lot better, and then more people would want it. Hmm. I say give them a meltdown!

It's very hard to do an intensive ABA program.

Many people find that they can't do it. Maybe they have a sick spouse, or other kids…there is an endless list of reasons why it's not possible, and people give in to the many reasons there are. That makes them human. I have no judgment against those people; it has to be a tough decision to make and even harder to live with it. But I have often seen something really disturbing. I have seen someone who couldn't do it try to talk someone else out of doing it. They tell the harrowing story of how it just isn't possible, how no one can possibly do a forty-hour-a-week program. I am guessing they do this because it feels better when others agree with you. Feel bad for people who couldn't do it, but don't let them talk you into not doing it. Yes, it's hard. I'm not going to candy-coat it. This is probably one of the toughest things you're ever going to do. Be proud of yourself when you make the decision to do it anyway. Surround yourself with people who have done it or are doing it. We will remind you that we didn't think we could do it either, but we did. It is possible. It is worth it.

Many people are judging ABA on what they think it is or what they think it was. They think they are right. The truth is they are thinking of something else.

My husband and I had a discussion about a movie the other day. I said I hated the movie. My husband was shocked. "I thought you loved that movie?" "No, I HATE that movie." We talked on and on. My son was there and eventually left the room about the time my husband realized I was thinking of a different movie with a similar title. Turns out I do love the movie he was talking about. We had been arguing about two entirely different things without realizing it, and if you asked my son now, he would tell you that I hate a movie I actually love, because he wasn't there when I realized the truth. What's my point? If someone starts telling you horrible things about ABA, go see it for yourself. They might be talking about a different movie.

The doctor who diagnosed my son with Autism, a fifty-year veteran in the field of Autism and pediatrics, a developmental pediatrician, made me promise in her office that I would not do ABA with my son. She convinced me it would turn him into a robot. Thank the lord above and butter pecan ice cream, I didn't listen to her for very long. My joke-telling, wise-cracking son is as far from a robot as you can get, although he a drew a robot that was featured on a line of t-shirts when he was eight! Don't listen to people who don't know what ABA is. Even when they look like an expert.

Don't just google ABA either. Chances are you will see a weird video, showing a kid at a table, with someone saying something really weird like, "Touch car," in a really robotic tone voice. Argggh! I hate those videos. Not to get too boring, but what those videos show is something called DTT. It is one step in the way something is taught, but it's not the whole picture. It would be like me explaining ballet to you by only ever showing you someone doing a plie in second position. It would get pretty boring pretty fast, and you would have no idea how a plie could grow into a series of movements that set to music could tell a story that would bring you to tears. What a shame if that silly plie was all you ever thought ballet was!

ABA is like a giant toolbox filled with amazing ways to teach. Over the years we have learned more and more about the behavior of learning and how to use the tools in new and better ways. People who are trained in how to design a program to use those tools are BCBAs (Board-Certified Behavior Analysts.) You should have one on your team; your insurance probably won't pay for therapy if you don't have one. The rest of the people on your team will be behavior technicians. Some of them might be RBTs (Registered Behavior Technicians) or BCATs (Board-Certified Autism Technicians). Some of them might be working for those credentials. By the way, you can become an RBT or a BCAT if you want to. Most of the training can be done easily online. Visit https://autismpartnership-foundation.org/free-rbt-training/.

Don't discount a behavior technician because they are new. All amazing therapists were once new. We all prefer to have the experienced "rockstar" technicians on our child's team, but this is a rookie mistake. What you want is a group of people who will help your child make the most progress, and that means a mix of people who are experienced and some who are not. WHAT? How can that be, Shannon?

Experienced behavior technicians are going to use the best tools in the best way to help your child learn, but the goal is not to have your child be able to demonstrate their skills to a trained therapist. The goal is to have them use their skills in the real world, amongst people who don't know ABA. The newer, less experienced people on your team are going to help your child, even when they aren't perfect. Sometimes their imperfections are going to make all the difference. I know; we all think, "I want my child to have the best!" and we love to see the progress a child makes with a veteran therapist. I couldn't get my child to come to me when I said, "Come here." But we had a rockstar therapist named Peter Farag come to our house, and within minutes he would say, "Come here!" and my son would walk right over to him. I decided Peter was a miracle worker and I only wanted Peter. Thank heavens Peter was an expert, because he explained to me that my thinking was upside down. The outcome I was praying and working for was my son being able to move about the world on his own, without support. I wasn't hoping for a world in which Peter went everywhere with my child. That wasn't the goal. So my son needed to learn from a lot of people, and he needed to be able to respond to people who had little to no training in ABA. Peter said to me, "Shannon, think of it this way: his teachers aren't going to know much about ABA, and someday, in fifth grade, his teacher is going to call in sick. The substitute teacher isn't going to know anything about ABA or even about Autism. We want your son to be successful on that day." So you need some rockstars on your team for sure, but you also need the new behavior technicians too. They know way more ABA than the teacher and worlds more than the substitute, and they are a nice transition for your child.

ABA is going to teach you how to be an amazing parent. It's going to improve your relationship with your child in ways you can't imagine. If you learn it and use it, it has the ability to change every relationship you have for the better.

Don't just drop your child off and hope that ABA will work its magic without you. Learn it, live it. Do everything you can to uphold what you learn every day. Forgive your-self when you are not perfect. No one is. Ever. Remember to reward yourself and everyone on your team for making the hard choice you are making and for following through on it. Walk tall. You are amazing.

One last word... for those of you who don't have access to ABA or to ABA funding...

There are ways that you can do an intensive ABA program on your own. It's hard, harder than hard, it's titanium, but it's possible. People have done it; you wouldn't even be the first. There are a couple of things you will need:

1. *Help.* You can't do this by yourself. You need at least one other person, preferably more. Otherwise, the child will learn to respond only to you. Generaliza-tion will be really difficult.

2. *Get trained.* If you're really going to do this, you have to become at least an RBT, and so will the other people on your team. The Autism Partner-ship Foundation offers free RBT training at https://autismpartnershipfoundation.org/free-rbt-training/

Say this or something like this:

I am a good parent. I have done my research and I have decided to follow the science and give my child their best oppor-tunity to learn and grow. I will learn from experts how to be a strong part of my child's team. I will not be the weakest member of the team. I will give myself the gift of knowing that I gave my child all that was possible. I will not settle for what is easy. I am a parent on a mission.

Resources

Granpeesheh, Doreen. *Evidence-Based Treatment for Children with Autism: The Card Model.* Academic Press, 2014.

"Board Certified Behavior Analysts (BCBA)." Behavior Analyst Certification Board, September 29, 2021, https://www.bacb.com/bcba/.

CHAPTER
5
Insurance

Welcome to the modern age of Autism, where therapy is funded by mainstream insurance. Can I pause for a second to tell you that on the day my son was diagnosed, I was told insurance would never pay for Autism therapy? Never. Not in my lifetime. Not in your lifetime. Not in our kid's lifetime! Then a group of parents in Arizona got together and even though THEY KNEW THEY WEREN'T GOING TO BE SUCCESSFUL, they began pushing their state legislators. They pushed and they started a revolution. I don't think anyone was more surprised than that group of parents when they got insurance to fund Autism treatment. Those parents changed the world.

Now here we are in the promised land. Insurance is now covering Autism treatments, including the Gold Standard: Applied Behavior Analysis. Wonderful, except that like in most promised lands, there is a lot of work to be done and very little is actually easy. Plus, there is a whole new set of jargon terms to learn! Yippee! This chapter is designed to cut through the crud to get to what is important: getting treatment.

First Things First

You are probably wanting to know: "Am I covered?"

The answer: Probably. Statistically speaking, you're more likely to have behavioral health coverage than not.

Action item: Pick an ABA provider, give them your insurance card, and ask them if you have coverage in your plan. They should be able to find this information for you.

Insider tip: If it takes them more than a week to find this out for you—a word to the wise—they are too busy and it will likely take you forever to start services. Look for another provider if possible.

Can you call yourself? Yes. We used to tell people to go in and talk to their benefits person in HR, but we quickly found that a lot of HR people didn't know anything about Autism coverage unless another family had already been through the process. Many parents have tried calling the number on the backs of their cards. This works sometimes, but mostly you are patched through to the least knowledgeable person who works for the insurance company. Too often you get an answer that doesn't accurately reflect the truth, and you've already wasted time. Your ABA provider talks to insurance companies all day. They should know who to call to get the right answer and cut through the red tape. It's also a great test to see how on their game they are.

If you find you have coverage, it is a great relief, but it's nowhere near the end of your insurance saga. Skip down to "Terms to Know"!

If you find you don't have coverage, don't panic. It's important to know why. Ask.

If You Are Told It's Because You Have a Self-Funded Plan

Technically a self-funded plan isn't actual insurance. It looks like insurance and acts like it's insurance, but it doesn't meet the definition of insurance, so it is not legally obligated to pay for behavioral health. You should know that many self-funded plans choose to cover ABA because it is the right thing to do. It is worthwhile to ask for a meeting to talk with your employer about their decision to NOT cover Autism therapy and what that will mean to you and your family. Be polite. Be respectful. Have your facts in a row. Document everything that is said by you and your employer. Many companies changed their ways after a respected employee shed light on the subject. Honestly, it happens all the time. It's possible. But don't hitch all your hopes to it.

Insider Tip: If you are not covered for any reason, apply for Medicaid in your state immediately. Beware, some

Medicaid programs have more than one choice. Call your ABA provider and ask them which one they accept. This is an important step. Don't try to bypass it.

If You Are Told You Don't Have Coverage Because of Your Child's Age

It is very likely illegal, even if you live in a state with age caps. There is a federal law, the Mental Health Parity and Addiction Equity Act (MHPAEA), that prevents age limits on one group if it is not on all groups. Federal law is always more powerful than state law. First ask your insurance company to give you written notice of why you are being denied services. Then call them and tell them they are in violation of the Mental Health Parity Act and you need your services started. If that doesn't work, appeal and appeal again. Get a lawyer if you need one.

Terms to Know

Premium: This is what you pay to have the privilege of insurance coverage.

Deductible: This is how much you pay before your insurance kicks in. When the deductible is met, that is when the insurance will pay. If you have a $2,000 deductible, you have to pay $2,000 before your insurance pays anything.

Copay: This is the dollar amount you pay for visits and services. Different services will cost a different amount; you might have a $20 copay for doctor visits and a $75 copay for an ER visit.

Out of Pocket Maximum: This is the total amount you have to pay in a given year before insurance has to cover everything.

I know—it's like gobbledygook, right? But this gobbledygook could be the thing that determines whether your child makes as much progress as possible and whether you will have an empty bank account, so stay with me... Let's shed a flashlight on this!

Spoiler Alert: The Out of Pocket Maximum Is the Most Important Number!

Let's take case A.
1. Premium: through the employer, $125.00 monthly for the whole family,
2. Deductible: $0
3. Copay: $25
4. Out of Pocket Maximum: individual $3,000, family $10,456

This family starts an early intensive intervention for their child.

Every month they pay $125 for premiums.

The child is getting therapy seven days a week. A $25 copay is billed every day, so each week the family owes: $175.

Meanwhile the child has other doctor's appointments, and they have a copay, so at the end of the first month, the family finds they have paid $1,100 in medical bills. That's not even counting the premium!

Mom thinks to herself. "We can't afford this! We need to cancel therapy! Maybe we should only have sessions two times a week. That's what my budget can afford!"

It makes sense, right?

NO, because mom isn't considering the Out of Pocket Maximum.

If things keep going the way they are, in less than three months this family will meet the out of pocket maximum, and when they do, they won't pay anything for the rest of the year. By the end of the year, the child will receive over $100,000 worth of therapy—exactly what was prescribed, and they did it for $3,000! That's not a bad deal. Or they could shortchange their child, still pay $3000, but get a lot less therapy. That's a bad deal. See the chart on the next page.

Month	Cost to family for therapy seven days a week	Cost to family for therapy two days a week
January	$1,000	$1,000
February	$1,000	$200
March	$1,000	$200
April	OOPM is met	$200
May	All therapy is free	$200
June	All therapy is free	$200
July	All therapy is free	$200
August	All therapy is free	$200
September	All therapy is free	$200
October	All therapy is free	$200
November	All therapy is free	$200
December	All therapy is free	OOPM is met

Total hours	1,920 hours of therapy	576 hours of therapy
Total cost	$3,000	$3,000
What insurance paid	$100,000	$2,000

If Mom stops therapy, the only winner is the insurance company. Don't even get me started on how much more progress an individual makes when they get more therapy. It's life-changing. So you can pay $3,000 and get everything your child needs, or you can pay $3,000, not give your child what was prescribed, and save the insurance company thousands of dollars. What do you choose? When you see it this way, doesn't it make sense to get more?

You might be thinking, "Shannon, that's all well and good, but I don't have $3,000 to start with!!!" I know. That is most people's story. You are not alone. Or left out. There are grants to help you. I have a whole chapter on that! Even if you aren't eligible for grants, call the ABA provider and ask them to put you on a monthly plan to pay copays. I can't guarantee they will work with you, but they should. It's good business. They benefit from you doing your full prescription too.

Let's take case B.

1. Premium is $885 a month
2. Deductible is $2,000
3. Copay: $0
4. Out of Pocket Maximum: $4,200 individual, $10,500 for whole family

So this family is paying $885 a month just to have coverage!

Their child has started ABA services and is getting forty hours a week. They don't have a copay, but their insurance doesn't start paying until they pay $2,000. At $50 an hour, the family will reach their deductible in the first week. Now the insurance will pay eighty percent, and the family must pay twenty percent until they reach $4,200 for the child or $10,500 as a family. Notice they will meet their OOPM in their second month.

We've already seen it doesn't pay to remove therapy hours, but let's see what it looks like for this family if they keep doing forty hours a week.

Month	Cost to family if doing forty hours of therapy a week
January	$3,200
February	$1,000
March	OOPM is met—No Cost Therapy
April	No Cost Therapy
May	No Cost Therapy
June	No Cost Therapy
July	No Cost Therapy
August	No Cost Therapy

Month	Cost to family if doing forty hours of therapy a week
September	No Cost Therapy
October	No Cost Therapy
November	No Cost Therapy
December	No Cost Therapy

Total hours	1,920 hours of therapy
Total cost	$4,200
What insurance paid	$99,800

Again, the idea of that $4,200 is very daunting, but ask your provider if they will let you make regular payments and apply for grants. There are some grants for $5,000.

I know it's overwhelming, but take a breath, because there is more.

What if you aren't starting in January? What if you are starting in October? And then what happens when you start a new year?

Make yourself a graph just like I did and start in the month you start. Know the rules of your insurance. They are usually stated right on the Explanation of Benefits that come with most statements. The whole cycle starts over in January. But knowledge is power. Usually when you are shopping for a plan, you think optimistically and look for a low copay or a low deductible, and you don't even glance at the out of pocket maximum. For Autism treatment, you are very likely looking at a minimum of two years where you will have to pay your out of pocket maximum. A smart shopper will ask when open enrollment is and compare policies to see which has the lowest OOPM paired with the lowest premium. Don't forget to confirm that your ABA provider will accept the insurance you have chosen.

Key things to do
1. Know your OOPM
2. Confirm your provider is in network for your insurance
3. Apply for Medicaid anyway. Apply under the grounds your child is disabled; in some states you have to apply first according to your income and be denied, and only then can you apply for your child under disability. It's a lot of hoops to jump through. Get a relative to help you, but do it. *In some states, Medicaid will pay your copay or whatever portion your insurance does not cover, potentially even your deductible.*

Read that last part again. You may not have to pay anything out of pocket. A significant percentage of parents cannot afford even the copays. If you can't, you are not alone. But notice it isn't a reason to give up. You know the old saying, "When there is a will, there's a way." Find your way. Ask for help. Ask other parents how they manage.

When all else fails, parents hold fundraisers to make up the difference. I write more about this in the finance chapter. Everyone is opposed to this in the beginning; I was too. But people actually love to donate to these kinds of things. When you explain to them that you are trying to raise $3,000 so your insurance will pay $100,000... what a great deal! Everyone loves making the insurance pay up! And a child gets better? You will be thrilled when you see how many people are excited to donate.

FAQ on Insurance

1. *My insurance doesn't have an in-network agreement with the treatment provider I want.*

   Ask the provider to help you request a "Single Case Agreement." If providers are few and far between where you live, you will likely be successful. If the insurance company has lots of providers near you, you will have to find a reason why the provider they assigned you isn't acceptable. Maybe their in-network providers have waiting lists and the provider you want can start you right away. Maybe their in-network providers only offer home-based services and you want center-based, etc. Make your case and be diligent.

2. *My insurance is asking for a reauthorization.*

You filled out all your paperwork, got it in, and then went through the arduous task of starting therapy; now it's three or six months later and the insurance company wants to reauthorize your insurance and get new paperwork? Yeah. Insurance has learned that all families don't take their intervention seriously. Maybe they gave you forty hours the first time, but you only used thirty. Now the insurance company is going to come back and authorize you for twenty-eight. Every few months they are going to check in to see if you still qualify for service and for how much. Is your child making progress, and do they still need therapy? It's a pain. Get used to it and beat them at their own game. Keep a place on your computer for all your Autism-related files. Scan documents you need frequently and keep them organized. Get all your paperwork in on the day it is requested, and then check to make sure it was received.

Let's not mince words here. The paperwork has the potential to bury you. The hoops you are forced to jump through will exhaust you. But the biggest hurdle is what goes on in your head. Your head may scream, "It's not fair. It's not reasonable. It's not rational to put parents through this and potentially cause their children to suffer as a result of this ridiculousness! It's maddening!" You may find yourself getting stuck in the anger, resentment, fear, and general state of overwhelm. You are entitled to all of your feelings, but all of your righteous indignation and resentments won't help your child reach their fullest potential.

Insider advice: Find a productive outlet for your feelings. Write, exercise, join a support group—whatever helps you to express your feelings and not get paralyzed in them. This isn't a one-size-fits-all. One parent may enjoy going to a gym and kickboxing the stuffing out of a punching bag; another parent may find blogging to be their perfect outlet. Do what works for you. Just try not to pick something that creates another problem. I tried to eat to deal with my frustration. Not a good plan.

I urge you to accept and express your feelings but accept that this is the deal for now and then take action. If you know you are going to have an insurance reauthorization every three months, accept it. Every minute you take arguing in your head that it's not fair is a minute you weren't getting the paperwork in. Insurance wins when we waste time arguing the injustices of it all. Even if it's only in our own heads. Don't fall in this trap!

Say this or something like this to yourself:

This paperwork sucks, but this is what I need to do to help my child. I am awesome because I'm going to get it done in record time and follow up on it. I'm capable of playing this game to get my child what they need. I'm not going to slow my roll just because of some paperwork! I do what needs to be done for my child.

Insurance is frustrating, and it requires a lot of attention. But it is also an amazing means to an end. A savvy parent who knows how to navigate the insurance craziness can access the highest level of care for their child. Be that parent.

Say this or something like this to yourself:

I am a $mart parent. I have taken the time to understand insurance so I can get maximum funding for my child. I am excited to think of how much therapy and support my child gets because I understand the system and use my knowledge to its full benefit!

CHAPTER 6

Medicines & Supplements

I am not a doctor. I don't even play one on TV. That is important to remember. A lot of people who aren't doctors are going to give you advice about medicines and supplements for Autism. Why is that? Because most doctors AREN'T going to give you advice or help with medicines and supplements for Autism. ARGH! What?

It's true. If you go to your run-of-the-mill board-certified, neighborhood pediatrician and ask him/her what supplements your child with ASD should be taking, you MIGHT, MIGHT, if you are lucky, hear a suggestion about taking a good probiotic...and then silence. Your average pediatrician does not have time to be up to date on the biomedical treatments for Autism, and if they start to wander that way, they will change their practice, become an expert, and charge 2x what they were charging before. Those experts are called MedMaps Doctors.[4] There are a growing number of them around the country. A few of them are pediatricians, others are immunologists, neurologists, etc...I would encourage you to know the full

4. http://medmaps.org

credentials of any doctor you work with. To find a Med-Maps Dr., visit their website, and always check that a doctor is in good standing with MedMaps before visiting with them.

Get ready, because it's going to be expensive, and it is likely that your insurance is not going to cover all of it, or potentially any of it. I really want to encourage you to join The Autism Community in Action (TACA) for a small yearly fee and get yourself a free TACA mentor. These are moms and dads who have been there/done that biomedically. They can advise you on which doctor you should see, how to spend your $ wisely, which tests to turn down—which supplements may have side effects, etc.

Here is my personal advice, which not everyone agrees with... When doing any biomedical intervention, only do one thing at a time. Give it at least thirty days unless there are terrible side effects and do not start anything else for at least thirty more days, sixty if you really want to be smart. So often, parents will put their children on ten different supplements all at the same time. Then the child gets a rash. Okay, which supplement was it? Nobody knows. Or the child suddenly is doing better in one area but struggling in another. Is it the supplements? Which one? I'll guess with you. It becomes a nightmare.

Sometimes there are supplements that will create adverse issues while the body adjusts, but that means they are working. When you are only adding one new supplement, this is easy to see and manage. If you have given a bunch of new supplements, you can never be sure if the reaction is positive/negative/temporary. It's frustrating, expensive, and sometimes cruel to the kids. Go slow. I know it feels bad, like you might be missing out on something huge, postponing progress, but that's why it's important to work with a TACA mentor. They will help you to put what you're going to try in a priority order so you will try the things that are more likely to help first.

One more word of advice on pharmaceuticals. There are some doctors who will rush to put children on traditional meds, things like respiradol. I want to wholeheartedly encourage you to make that your last resort after you have tried diet, behavior modification, and supplements. There are cases where, after attempting all of these things, a parent has still felt the meds were warranted, but in many of the cases I am aware of, parents have found that one or a combination of all of those things worked for their child and they did not need meds. There are side effects to the meds. It is worthwhile to try everything else first. Just my two cents. And if you are a parent who is currently giving your kids meds, it's not too late to go back and try a new diet, new therapy, and new supplements.

Having said all of this, I think it's important to note that individuals on the spectrum, like all people, will have medical needs throughout their lives. And there are medicines and supplements that are helpful to individuals on the spectrum.

I love listening to Dr. Doreen Granpeesheh, a licensed psychiatrist and a true expert in the field of Autism, talk about case studies where children made exponential progress in their behavior intervention plan after medical treatment for fungus, inflamed gut, or yeast overgrowth. Thank goodness more mainstream doctors, more behaviorists and more people are starting to realize that a comprehensive approach to autism treatment is more effective at meeting the individual needs of each person.

Say this or something like this to yourself:

My child is an individual, and they deserve individualized medical treatment. I am a fierce advocate for my child and their right to good medical treatment. I have the right to ask questions. I have the right to seek out a different doctor if I feel my concerns are not being addressed.

Resources

"About Us," *https://www.medmaps.org/about-us/.*

"Family Resources." The Autism Community in Action (TACA), May 28, 2021, https://tacanow.org/family-resources/.

CHAPTER
7
Grief

This chapter is about grief and anger and fear, all of which are connected, all of which are a part of being a parent of an individual with an Autism Spectrum diagnosis. You are allowed to grieve. It doesn't make you a bad parent. It doesn't mean that you don't love your child. It doesn't mean that you don't accept your child for who they are. It is the opposite, in fact. The grief is part of accepting that things aren't what you thought they were. Your life and your child's life isn't/aren't what you planned.

If you haven't read "Welcome to Holland,"[5] you need to. In the early days, it's really important to cut yourself some slack. All of the emotions you're feeling are valid.

Many of us have found ourselves crying about things that other people would find ridiculous. I cried for two days after my son was diagnosed because I kept picturing the dinner party I had been planning to have after he graduated from college. It was something I had started

---

5. Kingsley, Emily Perl. "Welcome to Holland." NDSS, July 24, 2020, https://www.ndss.org/lifespan/a-parents-perspective/.

planning at birth! Along came the diagnosis, and the image was completely shattered in my mind. My son was two and a half and I was crying about a college graduation party. If I had told anyone, they would have thought I was nuts. But that's what my brain could comprehend at the time. And it was sad.

My husband, when he finally got to the grief, which was a full six months later, found himself crying after seeing a play with a child actor. He said, "I just realized our son may never know the joy of being in a play or listening to a good piece of music." My husband wept like a baby. You can't judge whatever the feelings are or the story that comes with them. Just allow them. Don't bottle them up; that's when bad stuff happens.

Allowing the grief allows you a new perspective. It's like a good, hard spring rain, it's intense and dark, but when it's over, the sun comes out and you can see sprouts peeking out of the mud. Possibilities. Grief allows us to see what we won't give up on. I was able to see that the graduation party was something I could live without, but the feeling of pride in my son and knowing that I had helped him to be ready for an independent life—that I wasn't willing to give up on. It became my guiding principle. When stuff got tough, I would picture myself standing by my son in a cap and gown getting ready to graduate. I would look him in the eye and tell him that I was proud of him and that his dad and I did all that we could to help him. That image motivated me through things that I couldn't otherwise do. It kept me strong and on task.

My husband found that he could not live with the notion that his son would not fully enjoy the arts, and it became a focus for him and for us. It was essential that our son at least appreciate good art, theatre, and music. Our son has already been in two plays, and I was thrilled one summer when my husband and son went to see Ringo Starr at the Greek Theatre. I was a little nervous because I knew they would be playing a lot of music my son had never heard. Would he be bored, restless? Would he want to leave early? I got a message during intermission from my ecstatic husband; my son had turned to him and said, "This is really awesome!" Victories. Worked for and won, because we weren't willing to give up on them. All sprung from grief. So don't deny the grief; it's powerful.

Sometimes grief is too much to be borne and so we become angry. Anger is a very real part of this dance too. You are entitled to your anger too. I suggest you write about it and get really clear what you are angry about and whom, if anyone, you are angry at. Keep your writing private so you can be completely honest. Many of us find that as the layers pull back, we are actually a little angry at ourselves even. Guilt is often riding right below the anger.

Depending on what your beliefs are about how the universe works, you may even feel like Autism has come into your life because of something you did or did not do.

In modern civilization we tend to categorize everything as either good or bad, and if it is bad, our next question is whose fault is it? Let's be mad! Mad is easy. I would much rather be mad than sad. Mad has energy; when you are mad, there are things to do! Plots to plot, hate to spew. Sad feels defeated. There's no fun in that.

So I offer to you that there is a time and a place for the anger. It can help you to get through some of the really tough stuff, but be careful. It's easy to get stuck in anger, and anger is never a good long-term strategy. Whenever I feel myself in the anger pool, I try to go back to the notion of good and bad. If I am feeling anger, I have already decided something is bad. But is that the truth? The sticky truth is that there is very little that is just good or just bad. Most things and circumstances have elements of both. Acknowledging that often sucks the heat out of the anger, for me, and then I am left with the fear. Ahhh. The scary part.

We are all afraid. We are right to be afraid. The world is not always kind to our kids, and we are not going to live forever. Everybody, breathe. I know I just massively rocked the boat. Breathe. Yes, this is the thing that lurks in the shadows and steals our sleep. What will happen when I am gone? It is the open nerve. Little by little you are going to have to answer the question for yourself. You are going to come up with a plan that is fluid, that grows with your child. You are not going to let this thought paralyze you or steal the time you have with your child. You are going to create a map and build a world around that map. You are going to live in the solutions, not in the fear. Okay?

You are going to ask yourself positive assumptive questions, like: Where would I love to see my child live when he is an adult? Your mind might stumble, because it has to invent a place—that's okay! Let it invent a place! The place of your dreams! Get specific with it. Then you can go look for it in life, and if you don't find it, you can start to build it. Believe me, there will be other people looking to build it too. They will find you, you will find them—it will be right out of *Close Encounters of the Third Kind.* You might even want to sculpt something out of mashed potatoes! The point is this is how good things come to be. It starts with something that is unbearable, so unbearable that it requires a solution. Don't deny yourself the joy of working to better things because you didn't allow yourself to feel the grief, anger, and fear that come with this ride.

You might find that you are vehement about your child remaining at home and living with you...forever. People used to ask me what my plan for my son was after my death, and without missing a beat I would tell them

I was planning to live forever. I meant it, because anything else was unthinkable. Over the years I have met so many parents whose children no longer live with them. The solutions were as different as the individual families. Some kids have gone on to college, jobs, marriages, and parenthood...it happens. Some kids have gone to group homes, but not the group home of your nightmares. There are some amazing places out there that allow for a supportive environment while granting dignity and fostering independence. I think my favorite thing is seeing the relationship between the parent and the adult child flourish in this environment. Parenting doesn't end when your child moves out, and life doesn't end with an Autism Spectrum diagnosis. Everyone continues to grow. One mom in particular told me that allowing her son to leave home and live in assisted living was the greatest gift she could ever give her son. She told me that when she leaves this planet, she knows her son will miss her, but he won't have to miss her and transition to living somewhere else at the same time. He's already made that transition, and she got to be there to smooth out the rough spots with him. It may be unthinkable now, but someday your child isn't going to live with you. How do you want to plan for that day to be successful? I think we can all agree it's best to do it while you are alive.

Say this or something like this:

I am entitled to all my feelings. I do not need to label my feelings "good" or "bad," and I don't have to justify them to anyone. I do not allow my feelings to prevent me from taking action. I allow my feelings to be, but not to become me.

Resources

Kingsley, Emily Perl. "Welcome to Holland." NDSS, July 24, 2020, https://www.ndss.org/lifespan/a-parents-perspective/.

"Books." The Work of Byron Katie, April 13, 2021, https://thework.com/books/.

C H A P T E R

8

Dealing with Questions

People are going to ask you questions, and for your own sake I would encourage you to formulate your stock answers. Keep them short and to the point, like media talking points. You will find that your answers will change with time—that's good. Your answers should be personal to you and your family. I have given a list of FAQ below and given my stock answers and two others; see if you can guess which is my answer. You should feel free to write your own version in the space provided.

What is Autism?

1. It is a neurological difference. It's like having a different operating system. Like the difference between a Mac and a PC.
2. It is a developmental disability that impacts communication and social skills.
3. It is a spectrum of disorders that can have a huge impact on someone's life or only mildly affect them.

Do they know what causes Autism yet?

1. No. But we know that it is definitely part hereditary and part environmental insults.
2. The current theory is that epigenetics effect development of the brain. Immune response may play a role.
3. Genetics loads the gun, and the environment pulls the trigger.

Is your child high-functioning?

1. Yes. (Regardless of your child's current skill level, why not answer it affirmatively?)
2. I don't subscribe to those terms because it requires context. One person might be great in the kitchen but a wreck on the ski slope. So would they be high-functioning?
3. What do you mean by high-functioning?

Why aren't you punishing him for that behavior?

1. We are doing a scientifically based intervention that has been proven to work. Thanks for your support.
2. I will punish him later when you aren't here. (Lie.)
3. We tried punishing him for that, and it didn't work. Now we are trying something else. I'll let you know if it works.

Is there really an increase in the number of cases of Autism or are they just getting better at diagnosing it?

1. Yes.
2. No.
3. They are getting better at diagnosing it, but there is a definite increase in the cases of Autism worldwide.

Didn't they prove that vaccines don't cause Autism?

1. They have proven that vaccines are safe for most children, but the US vaccine court has paid out claims for children that have been injured by vaccines and developed Autism, so there are still some unanswered questions.
2. I don't know. I'm not a doctor. What do you think?
3. That is the current mainstream scientific consensus, but there seem to be a lot of parents who still aren't satisfied with that answer.

It's so sad that so many of these people have Autism. Isn't it sad?

1. No. I know lots of people on the spectrum, and they are beautiful individuals.

2. I would rather have a child who is kind and on the spectrum than a child who is mean to children with challenges.

3. I'd rather talk about all the things they can do—let's talk about "This Ability," not disability.

The point is people are going to say things to you that are going to try your patience. You can get mad at them or you can create some fun answers for yourself that empower you and your kid. I encourage you to only speak positively about your child to your child, and part of that is speaking positively about them to the world. At the end of the day, always be on your child's side. Make it the rule and you can never go wrong.

Say this or something like this to yourself:

I choose to be an advocate for my child. Some people are ignorant about Autism and the challenges my child faces. It is not my job to fix them. It is my job to love my child, take their side, and be their champion.

CHAPTER
9

Friends, Family & People You Want to Stick in a Cuisinart

People are going to offend you, say stupid things, and hurt your feelings. It's going to happen. I'm sorry. I realize I sound cynical, but I'm right. It's going to happen, and if you know it's coming, you might be better prepared than if you just get sucker punched.

People don't mean to be stupid and hurtful, but they are ignorant. We were once ignorant about Autism too, so we can't really hold it against people when they don't know something. We just have to decide: is it worth it to try to educate them? Your answers are going to change based on the day, your mood, the person you're talking to, and a whole host of other factors. This is a "choose your battles" kind of game. So when your Aunt Martha whom you see once every three years says to you at your cousin's wedding, "He doesn't have Autism; you just spoil him." You might decide to clench your fist, change the subject, and simply ask how your Uncle Mort's cataract surgery went. My personal rule of thumb is: how much time is my child going to spend with this person in the next two years? If the answer is almost none, then that is the amount of energy I am willing to spend to enlighten them. If my son's teacher had said that comment—whole other ball game. Her ignorance will impact my kid on a daily basis, so I need to get in there and do some work. Hopefully a teacher would not disavow a diagnosis; if they did, I would seriously look at moving classrooms.

My point is you don't have time to fix all the stupid stuff people are going to say to you. You have a choice, you can get really upset about it (not fun, I've done it), or you can sharpen your sense of humor on them (more fun, I've definitely done it).

I collect the stupid stories and share them at parties to intimidate people—they are afraid to say something stupid for fear I will share it at the next party.

My favorite is the woman who saw me talking to my son at the bottom of a bouncy house slide. He was little, probably four years old. It was a birthday party, it was loud, and there was chaos at the top of the slide. I wanted him to be safe, so I was giving him instructions and he was excited, so he wasn't making good eye contact. I had to tell him three times to focus and look at me before he could do it. I gave him his instruction and sent him up the slide. She immediately came over with her large butt-insky nose and said, "Is he sick? Because if he's sick, he shouldn't be here."

I said, "I beg your pardon?"

"He look's sick to me. If he's sick, he shouldn't be here," she said loudly. Now I was pissed.

"He's not sick," I told her.

"Are you sure he's not coming down with a cold? He looks glassy-eyed, and he wouldn't look at you when you were talking to him."

OHHHHH! She was just ignorant. In her world, if you don't look at someone, it means you are coming down with a cold. Oh. So I laughed at her.

"He doesn't have a cold. He has Autism."

To which Miss Ignoramus replied, "Autism, really? Gosh you would never know!" at which point I walked away, shaking my head.

She wasn't worth my time.

When a friend said to me, "You're so lucky your son has Autism; you get all that free child care," I had to make a decision. At first I let it go; maybe it was a one-time thing.

Then she said something else about how much easier parenting was for me, with only one child, and he has autism, so you get all that help, you barely have to do anything. I stopped her and had a very polite conversation about how wrong she was, and I detailed some of the things that she couldn't have known. I felt really good about the conversation. I felt like I had made a difference.

But the comments didn't stop, and the relationship became strained. For that and other reasons, we don't spend much time together anymore.

Which comes to the hard truth. All of your relationships aren't going to survive Autism. Some people are not going to be able to accept your new life and your new priorities. It's going to feel sad and harsh, but you're going to have to let go of those people. You might find they come back around, but you also might find that you outgrow them quickly. Honestly, imagine if someone in your family were diagnosed with a brain tumor and you lost a friend because they couldn't accommodate your new chemo schedule. They would be a pretty shallow friend, right? How is it any different if they can't accommodate your new Autism schedule? It's not different.

Having a child on the spectrum is going to reveal to you the people in your life who are capable of letting some things not be about them. In other words, the adults. Autism is going to show you who the adults are in your life. Cling to them. Together, wave to the children in adult bodies that go floating by. You aren't going to have time to take care of them, so wave goodbye now. Again, nothing is permanent, and if you want to reconvene with them later, you can, but don't be surprised if your life just works better without them!

I remember a pivotal moment for me. My son was in a classroom with a little boy my son referred to as a friend. The only problem was that every time they went on the playground, this little boy would try to hurt my son. He pushed him, shoved him, knocked him down, and even pulled the strings on my son's hood and tried to choke him. For me this was a real crisis. I was terrified the other boy was going to hurt my son. Everyone was involved in working on it from every direction. We taught my son how and when to yell for help. We also taught him to say, "STOP. You're hurting me and I don't like it!" to the other boy. The school worked with the other little boy to teach him better ways of getting my son to play with him. We tried everything, and yet the kid was still trying to hurt my kid. Not okay. Finally, the decision was made to separate the boys. My son missed his friend. He actually liked this little boy, despite the fact the kid was trying to hurt him. I found myself sitting on a bench with my son and trying to explain to him why he couldn't spend time with his "friend" anymore. I told him that sometimes friends will do something to hurt you, because sometimes there are accidents. But if your friend is hurting you and you ask them to stop and they don't, they aren't really your friend. I said this to my seven-year-old son with ASD and a limited grasp on the English language. And he seemed to get it. If you tell a friend they are hurting you and they keep doing it, they aren't a friend. I realized in that moment that I had at least one person in my life who was saying and doing things that were hurting me, my family, and my livelihood. I had asked them to stop, and they hadn't. I had made excuses. I had stayed friends with them. But in explaining it to my son, it had become clear to me. I knew this person wasn't really my friend. It was time to move on. I had told my son it was okay to be sad about saying good-bye to a friend and it was okay to miss them. He accepted that, so I told it to myself. Now I am telling it to you.

Is there someone in your life who is trying to hurt you? Ask them to stop. A true friend will stop. If they don't stop, do yourself a favor and move on.

You owe it to yourself and your child. Let's not forget you are trying to do something extraordinary. You are attempting to show up for your special needs child in a way that is meaningful. That is enough. You don't need someone else's baggage weighing you down. You have permission to let go of people and things that are holding you down.

Say this or something like this:

I am a good person and a good parent. I am allowed to have boundaries and to maintain them. When I maintain my boundaries with friends and family, I am teaching my child how to have boundaries. This is a loving way that I am teaching my child to have meaningful friendships.

CHAPTER
10
Finances, Funding & Grants

I t would be more appropriate for me to read this chapter than for me to write it. This is not my forte, and more than anything I hope you make better choices and have better solutions than I had, because I definitely screwed the pooch here. But here is what I need to say to you. I am 100 percent certain that we could not afford to do what we did. Yes, California paid for our therapy, but one parent had to be at home in order for our child to receive therapy. So our combined income halved at a time when we had more expenses as a result of Autism. It was rough. Whenever I crunched the numbers, it was clear that we weren't going to make it. Through a series of miracles, we kept a roof over our heads and food on the table. No matter what happened, we never gave up, and we always kept our priority as therapy. I could tell you all the things that went wrong and the messes we are still cleaning up, but it wouldn't matter. We did what we had to do, everything we had to do, anything we could do, just short of anything illegal. I have no regrets. I would rather be in debt and never own my own home but know in my heart that we did everything we could for our son. Having said that, if you are smart, you may find it doesn't have to be financially devastating to help your child.

Now with Center-Based ABA, the challenges are different. Both parents can work if the employer has some flexibility. Whatever you do, don't give up on therapy because of money. Get inventive. Apply for grants, seek out funding sources, hold a fundraiser, start a GoFundMe account, borrow from a rich relative…Make it happen. You won't be sorry unless you don't do it.

Here is the other thing: keep asking questions. Ask every parent you know what they know and how they are making things work. Yeah, it might be uncomfortable, but going bankrupt is uncomfortable too.

Don't accept one person's answer.

On one of our darkest days, I took my small, nonverbal (at that time) child and went to the local office I was told could help me apply for benefits. I arrived at 8 am and I left shortly after 5:30 PM that night when they were locking the doors. I spent the day filling out papers, standing in line, and then meeting with people who would tell me we didn't qualify for program after program. We didn't even qualify for food stamps. Not because of income. We qualified under income, but we were disqualified because we had two cars! We lived in Los Angeles. My husband was working, I was taking my son to therapies! We needed two cars. I didn't see how we could do my son's treatment with just one car, but it did mean we were disqualified for any support. I begged and asked, is there anything else? No. We managed by the skin of our teeth and I worked from home doing a million different things. It was hard. Sometimes it was impossible.

Years later I found out about a program that would have paid me up to $4,000 a month to take care of my child. A state program that we were qualified for. I never heard about it. I listened to one woman, and I stopped asking questions. She didn't know about the program. She wasn't trying to be mean. She just didn't know. No one knows everything. Keep asking questions. In a previous chapter I suggested you apply for Medicaid for your child. Each state has different Medicaid waivers, and it is so confusing! Look for the parent who seems to have it figured out. Ask questions. I have seen parents turn their entire lives around when they find the right waiver and are able to fully fund their child's program without fear of financial ruin.

Learn how to ask for and accept help. This is hard for a lot of us. Do it anyway. Make a list of your assets. I'm not just talking about property. If you have a friend who is supportive and willing to babysit one day a week, that is an asset! It's helpful to remind yourself of your assets. It creates a feeling of well-being and helps you to lean into the best parts of your life.

Use your assets well. There are grants you can apply for. Different grants for different things. One grant might pay for an iPad, another for copays, and a third might let you decide how to use the money. Get $mart and utilize your grant funds properly to get the biggest bang for your buck.

Say this or something like this to yourself:

There is no dollar sign over my child's head. They are price-less. Helping support them and the services they need tran-scends monetary value. I am $mart and relentless. I will learn from others, and I won't allow money to be a reason why my child doesn't make the progress they deserve.

Resources

United Healthcare Children's Foundation
http://www.uhccf.org/apply/

This 501(c)(3) non-profit charity gives grants up to $5,000 to help families gain access to medical-related services. You DO NOT have to have United Healthcare Coverage to apply, but there are other requirements. I have seen many families successfully get this grant for copays and other medical bills.

Autism Care Today!

http://www.act-today.org/

This non-profit organization helps families receive grant money for technology, equipment, therapies, copayment assistance, and more. Funds are limited, so take the time to write a personal letter where noted in the application.

Autism Speaks

https://www.autismspeaks.org/financial-autism-support

This is a comprehensive list of resources to help with all financial needs, including rent.

iTaalk

https://www.itaalk.org/grant-and-funding-source-list

This links to a comprehensive list of funding sources that are both Autism- and Non-Autism-specific.

KNOWAutism

https://know-autism.org/apply-for-assistance/

This organization provides funding for tuition and diagnostic assistance as well as special-case items like summer camp.

CHAPTER
11
Work

Unless you are independently wealthy, chances are you are going to have to keep working while your child goes through therapy and progresses through their life. Work and family are always a juggling act; now you are going to add in Autism. It's important to remember that even the best jugglers drop balls from time to time. Start now to set your priorities and lower some of your expectations. First of all, if there are two of you working, whose job is the most important and whose job is the most flexible? When one of you has to call in sick because your child has the sniffles, who is going to be able to do it making the fewest waves? Is it better for you to keep your jobs, or is it time to look for other work? Some of the things you need to consider are:

1. **How much time are you spending commuting?**
   Your time is at a premium right now. If you are spending hours commuting it may be time for a change.

2. Is this job hard to come by?

If you are in a job that is difficult to get, try really hard to make it work before you consider letting it go. The vast majority of jobs are changeable. Do a quick online search of your job title or description. Are there lots of jobs listed or almost none?

3. Is your job flexible with time or is it strictly 9-5?

Some employers are thrilled when workers ask for flexible time. For some it solves a staffing need, for others it is a really clear way of retaining good staff that is inexpensive! And then there are the jobs in which, by their very nature, flexibility is impossible. Those jobs may prove difficult for the long run.

4. Are there opportunities/expectations for overtime?

It's just a reality for some jobs: you have to put in overtime when they ask. If your significant other can't handle the home obligations by themselves, this may not be an option for you. It's good to communicate and set expectations.

5. Is your job stressful?

By this point you have probably figured out there is a fair amount of stress that comes with having your child diagnosed with Autism Spectrum Disorder. There is even a well-known study that has documented the stress as being akin to that of a person in combat. This annoys many people because they assume the stress comes from the child or the diagnosis. I can tell you it doesn't. It comes from all the things you have to do to fight for your child, their rights, and the services and therapies that will help them. The point is it's going to be stressful—do you really want to add a stressful job into the mix? I would encourage you to do whatever you can to manage and reduce stress on every level of your life, including your job.

6. *Do you love your job?*

If you love your job, fight for it...but don't let it get in the way of your child's progress. No matter how much you love it, I'm confident you love your child more.

7. *Does your workplace allow for people to job-share or work from home?*

A worldwide pandemic has changed this equation. It might be worth it to ask your employer what your options are. Can you work from home? If you come in late one day, can you stay late the next day to make it up? Knowing your parameters will be really helpful.

8. *Do you work on commission?*

Be very mindful if you are in a commission-only job. Remember at the beginning of the chapter we talked about how hard it is to keep all the balls in the air all the time. Commission only equals stress and that is without Autism. Use caution.

9. *Do you have good benefits?*

I know lots of parents who have stayed ten years longer in a job they didn't love because the job had benefits that allowed their kid to get good therapy. There are worse reasons for staying in a job.

The key is to make conscious decisions. If it makes sense to stay in the job you are in, then do what you need to do to stay in good standing with that job. If you need to take an occasional day off, make sure you meet your deadlines on other days. Plan ahead and ask for help. If there is a month that is particularly hard at your job and that requires extra attention, maybe that's the month your mother can visit and help out at home. Do what you have to do to keep a job that helps you get through this. Jobs that aren't flexible, that have sucky benefits, and that think you should work around the clock with no perks? Keep those jobs only until you can find the other kind.

Keep in mind that your employer can't legally fire you because you have a child on the Autism spectrum. If you need time off to go to clinics or IEP meetings, they have to allow you to do it. The smart thing is to tell your employer what is happening and then document any pushback you get from them on technology that is not tied to your work.

That means emailing your significant other from your private email account. Create a Gmail account if you don't have one and detail what was said to you and how it made you feel.

For instance:

> *Hey Honey,*
>
> *I'm super stressed. I told my boss I need to take next Tuesday off to take Billy to his clinic. I told him that it was a medical necessity and he told me if he let every parent take off to go to dental appointments we would never make our deadlines. I reminded him that our son had a disability, not a toothache. He says he just can't clear it this month. I'm sitting at my desk and I can feel my blood pressure rising. I know I need to go to clinic, but I don't want to lose this job either.*

Let me be clear. This is not about making something up. It's about documenting the truth. The law is on your side, but if lawyers end up getting involved, you will wish you had documentation.

There are many companies who have embraced their Autism families. I hope you are in a job like that or that you find one. There are those who choose never to disclose their child's diagnosis at their workplace. This is certainly a personal choice. It always make me sad when parents feel like they have to keep their child's diagnosis a secret. Don't get me wrong, sometimes it is necessary, but wouldn't it be nice if we lived in a world where we didn't have to worry about people discriminating against our children or our families because of an Autism diagnosis?

The most important thing to remember is finding the balance. You have to have income and your child has to have therapy. You've got to find the way it works; don't settle for less. The therapy won't be forever. Jobs do not define us or our children.

Say this or something like this:

I am okay. My child is okay. For this period of time, I am doing something brave and prioritizing my child's treatment. I am making compromises where I need to and changing what has to be changed to make this happen. This won't be forever. But it will be worth it.

CHAPTER
12
Love & Marriage

People tell me all the time that the divorce rate among people with special needs children is higher than the average divorce rate. And I hear that once you are divorced with a special needs child, there is no chance of ever finding love. I guess there are some studies that seem to point in these directions. I don't really buy into that. For me it's more how you look at things.

Marriage is hard; anybody who tells you different is blowing smoke up your tushy area. It's hard, and it takes two people willing to do the heavy lifting. One can't do it by themselves. Being a special needs parent is hard, really hard...but it is a hell of a lot easier doing it with a partner. If you and your partner can get into that mind-set, it gets easier. If you aren't with somebody who can do it with you, I'm really sorry. Forgive yourself; it's not your fault. Forgive them, mainly because being angry at them won't help. If you do have someone who is willing to slog it out with you, cling to them. Make it work. Focus on the good stuff and let everything else go by the wayside. It is the best gift you can give your child, so if it's possible, make it possible. Get therapy, get help, do whatever it takes.

For those of you who have already left, or have been left or know that you have to go …it doesn't mean that love is dead forever. I offer up the Paskowitz-Asners as a case in point.

Matt Asner was divorced with two kids, one on the spectrum. His plate was full. Between his career, kids, and advocacy for individuals on the spectrum, he didn't have time for anything, let alone love. Then he met Navah Paskowitz. She was divorced with four kids, two on the spectrum. Navah wasn't looking for love; she was looking for help for her youngest son. Matt and Navah met, he helped her find what she needed for her son, and then love flourished. Love so big that everyone who is around them gets diabetes. Between them now, they have six kids, three on the spectrum, and they are busy people together running the Ed Asner Family Center. They found love. If it's possible for them, it's possible for you. So don't give up on love, no matter what.

Some of the best advice I ever got on how to stay married while being a parent of a child on the spectrum came from none other than Dr. Temple Grandin. I had interviewed her, and we were all done. The cameras and lights were being packed up, and she started asking me about my husband and my son. She asked if my husband and

I ever took time to be together alone and not talk about Autism. I laughed so hard I looked like a Muppet, with the top of my head bobbing backward. When I could breathe, I told her I didn't even know what that would look like! Temple spent the next twenty minutes talking me through how I could logistically make time to be with my husband without our child and not worrying about our child. It was amazing, and at one point she could see that I had stopped paying attention, so she stopped and asked me where my head was at. Talk about social skills! I was honest and told her that I was having a surreal moment where my head was realizing that I was getting really good marriage advice from Temple Grandin. She laughed and said, "I'm really good at solving problems; it's what I do. It doesn't matter what the problem is." I loved that. I'm still not great at taking Temple's advice, but she put it on my radar, and I gave my relationship with my husband more time.

It also made me think about all the things we managed to do right. We had a rule in our house that when the last therapist left for the day, we would close the door and dance as a family for at least a minute. Sometimes it was to music, sometimes we sang, sometimes it was to whatever happened to be on the TV at that moment. I didn't realize at the time what a good thing that was. When the therapy stopped, we stopped dancing. Occasionally one of us will bring that up and suggest we do it again. It never happens. It was something magical, in the middle of something hard, that helped us all survive.

My husband and I always chose to have each other's backs too. That wasn't always easy. But we stood up for each other in public. I never threw him under the bus to my family or the therapists, and he never went to work and talked about me like I was a ball and chain. I credit my husband with that. He came home from work one day after listening to a coworker complain about their spouse for six hours straight, and he said he would like it if we never did that. So we did our best to make sure we didn't "tell on each other," and we admitted it when we did. I still come home some days and admit to him if I "told on him" during the show. I have his permission to tell some of the realities now so others can learn, but while we were going through it, we kept it positive.

The other very important thing I did was not letting my husband fuzz out. He wanted to, I WANTED to, but we couldn't. Whenever I would see him getting distant or starting to check out, I would get in his face and tell him he couldn't. That wasn't easy. Let's face it: it's easier to just check out yourself, and I wanted to. It wasn't an option. I didn't let it be an option.

The stereotype is that the moms with kids on the spectrum get really motivated and sink their teeth into everything related to Autism, while the dads get really busy at work and drift away. It isn't always that way, sometimes it's the moms who drift away. Sometimes the moms get so involved in Autism that they aren't around for the family. I walk a tightrope with that one now. Being distracted by something else is really comforting. Both people in a couple have to keep an eye on it and tug on each other when they start to drift. Not easy, but it sure beats doing it alone.

By the way, Temple's advice:

> Find another couple with a kid or kids on the spectrum and trade date nights. One night you get to go out with your spouse while they have all the kids, and the next time you watch the kids while they go out.

She also suggested having no expectations on the time spent together. She told me about a dad who confessed to her that their church had a once-a-month event where the kids with special needs could be dropped off so the parents could have a date. This dad admitted that he and his wife never actually left the parking lot. They would put the seats back, put on some soothing music, and sleep in their car. Temple insisted this was a better use of time than strategizing your child's healthcare. She insisted that it was essential to find time to simply "BE" with the other person.

I told you it was great advice. It's just easier said than done.

Say this or something like this to yourself:

I deserve to be in a loving relationship, and I welcome that energy in my life. I make time for myself and my relationships because they add meaning to my life and set an example for my child.

CHAPTER
13
School & the Dreaded IEP

School: it can either be great or it can be your biggest headache. If your child has an Autism Spectrum Diagnosis, they are entitled to an Individualized Education Plan (IEP). Most schools will tell you that they need to test your child in order to have an IEP. Let them test your child. But you can set parameters, what tests, how long they can test, when they test, who tests, where they test, who is present, etc.

Truth Alert

I am not aware of a single school district that has the funding to give every child what they need to be successful, so often schools give services to the squeakiest wheels. It is horrifying to think that as you advocate for your child to get good services at school, the reality is you may be taking those services away from another child. It's horrifying. Is it any better if you don't advocate for your child and let the other kid get the services? NO. Your child is your responsibility. If you don't advocate for them, no one else will. It is your job to be a squeaky wheel for your child.

Later, after you have helped your child, you can go back and help as many other children as you would like, but right now you need to do right by your kid.

That means:

- Do Not allow the school to change your IEP to a 504 plan. An IEP is a legal document that requires schools to give services; a 504 plan doesn't require the school to give any services, just accommodations.

- Do Not allow the school to do pull-outs during essential learning times. The school may offer your child speech, occupational therapy (OT), or adaptive physical education (APE) services and then take that child out of math class to perform these services. The child gets behind in math and eventually has to go to another classroom, school, or program. Argue for "push-in" services whenever possible and get it written in your IEP that "pull-outs" can't happen when you don't want them to.

- Do Not allow the school to segregate your child unless you feel it is best for them for a specific period of time. Your child is entitled to accommodations in the "Least Restrictive Environment" (LRE). Don't let the school shove your child into a special day class if a regular class with an aide would make more sense. The school is not allowed to say that money is an issue, so they will attempt to make other excuses. Be strong. Be willing to get legal support.

- Do Not allow the school to make decisions without you. You are a part of your child's IEP team. Don't ever let the school forget that.

Things to do to create a great IEP and a positive school experience:

1. Volunteer at your child's school and in your child's classroom. You will learn a lot, you will be informed, AND you will make allies with teachers, secretaries, staff, and other students. It all helps! It can be something fun. For years I directed the school play at my son's school, even when it didn't include his grade. I got to know the teachers and the students. It was fun, and I saw the kids on the playground be nicer to my son because they knew me. Hands down, the best use of time! Maybe directing the school play isn't your thing. Maybe you're great in the copy room and can volunteer time to help teachers get their materials ready. It doesn't matter what you do; be helpful. It will pay off.

2. Always attend IEP meetings and let them know in writing you will be recording it. Now you can record on your smartphone easily, so there is no reason

not to. You will find that when there is a record-ing, everyone, including you, will be on their best behavior. It will be very civil; you need to make sure you are civil. If you feel the need to yell, ask for a break; don't let it be on the recording. Parents tend to get squeamish about recording. They worry that the school will think they are being difficult. I have sat on both sides of IEPs; believe me, teachers and administrators respect parents who are strong advo-cates for their kids. Do yourself a favor and record. Schools make mistakes, and when we catch them in a mistake, it saves everyone time and money. Recording also puts an end to ridiculousness. Par-ents tell me some of the outrageous things said to them in IEPs. I ask if it was recorded, and the answer is too often no. Record, but notify the school at least forty-eight hours before the start of the meeting. I suggest getting in to the habit of responding to the invitation to the IEP by saying something like:

"Yes. I will be attending. Please let this serve as my official notification that I will be recording the meeting. Please email me any reports that will be referenced in the meeting 48 hours before the meeting." (see below)

3. Take the time to know what you want before going into an IEP meeting. I ask for all of the reports and recommendations that will be given at the meeting to be emailed to me forty-eight hours before the meeting so I can have time to review them. I ask for this in writing when I respond to the invitation for the IEP. Look, they don't always comply, but when they do, I read them and am better prepared for the actual meeting. The night before the meeting, I write a letter that lists all of the things I am asking for. I give compliments when they are due. I state clearly why I am asking for what I am asking for and tell why it is appropriate. Then when it is my turn to speak at the meeting, I read the letter. No matter what has happened, I read the letter. This way I don't have to be nervous or worry that I am going to leave something out, or worse, chicken out of saying something that I wanted to say but now I'm not sure about. I just have to read. Then I sign the letter in front of them and hand it over to them. I am clear in what I am asking for.

4. Show kindness, compassion, and the ability to be reasonable along with strength. I used to be a teacher, so I know how crazy things can get for a teacher. I always want to let a teacher know that I will support them if they are demonstrating a desire

to teach. There will be people in school settings who will severely test your patience. Always remember you will catch more flies with honey than with vinegar.

5. Get/put it in writing. Create a place where you can store all school communication. If someone says they are going to do something, ask them to put it in writing. If it isn't in the IEP, it's not legally binding. When you talk to someone, send them an email afterward.

> Ms. Thomas, as per our discussion today, I want to reiterate that Madison is not to be taken out of Math class to participate in speech services. Sincerely, One On-It Mom!

6. Start to familiarize yourself with your rights and your child's rights. You would think that schools and school officials would be up on these rights and upholding them. You would think that, and you would be wrong. Make it your business to know your rights, and you will find your child getting a better educational experience.

The school thing is a serious tightrope act. On the one hand, you want to be nice to anyone you think might have interactions with your child, but on the other hand, you have to show that you are the parent they don't want to mess with. Be willing to go toe-to-toe with anyone for the sake of your kid.

I hope you have good teachers (more on that in the next chapter), but don't assume that everyone deserves your trust. Make them earn it. If your kid is exhibiting weird or challenging behavior before school or after school, do whatever you have to do to find out what is going on and make sure your kid is safe.

I know parents who have sent a tape recorder to school in their kid's pocket. Now that is clearly illegal, and I would NEVER advise you to do that. But I can understand why parents do. Those parents are braver than I am. If I thought someone was hurting my kid, I wouldn't send them back to that school. I just couldn't. Not even with a tape recorder. I would pull my kid out. Or I would go with him. I would be the biggest pain in the neck.

I love Holly Robinson Peete. The first time I interviewed her, she said, "When the people in the office see you coming down the sidewalk to your child's school, if they don't say, 'Uh oh, here she comes!' then you aren't doing your job!" I took that as seriously as a heart attack. I suggest you mentally change your middle name to "On It" and live up to it at your child's school. Be a presence. It's hard, especially when you have other kids. Do the best you can and don't be afraid to change everything if it isn't working out. My biggest regret is the year I spent trying to work it out with a teacher whom I kept giving the benefit of the doubt. My child has had some of the best teachers there are, and that one year with a teacher who wasn't one of them did so much damage to his self-esteem that it took years to fix it. Don't be patient. Ask for corrective action, and if you don't see immediate results, ask for a new teacher.

Say this or something like this:

My child has a right to a Free Appropriate Public Education (in the US). My child deserves to be treated with dignity and to be given the opportunity to learn. The law is on my side. I will advocate for my child's needs and get help when needed to ensure they have access to good education.

Resources

"Wrightslaw." Wrightslaw Special Education Law and Advocacy. Accessed October 11, 2021. https://www.wrightslaw.com/.

"Individuals with Disabilities Education Act (IDEA)." Individuals with Disabilities Education Act, September 30, 2021. http://idea.ed.gov/.

"About COPAA - Council of Parent Attorneys and Advocates, Inc." Accessed October 11, 2021. https://www.copaa.org/page/about.

C H A P T E R
14

Therapists, Teachers & Other People Who Mean Well

You're going to start to look at the world in two groups: people who are on our side and people who aren't on our side.

There are going to be a lot of people who want to help you. They are going to mean well and show up with great intentions. Be kind to them. You need them. But don't make the mistake of abdicating to these folks and letting them take your place as the team leader. Because as much as these folks know, they still need you to be the place where the buck stops. Along the way will be decisions that need to be made, and there won't be a clearly defined right or wrong answer—there may be no wrong answer at all. You need to be the final say. You need to be the one who brings it all together in the end. In the beginning, it's going to feel odd. These people are the experts; maybe they should decide? Trust me: if you do that, you are going to end up feeling resentful and pushed around. No, you need to be the final say.

Be a benevolent leader, let the team know how much their work means, and you will find that you will always be surrounded by good people. Put your gratitude in writing. Write thank you notes and share them with your team's bosses. Write letters of recommendation for good teachers and ask for them to be included in their permanent file. Take the time to show your appreciation for the people who show kindness to you, your child, and your family. It will feel good.

Fire people who clearly aren't on your side, aren't doing their jobs, and aren't capable of doing their jobs. FIRE THEM! As disappointing as it is, there are people who are in this field simply because it is a job, and they are hoping to have to do as little as possible to get a paycheck. Shockingly, there are fewer of these people than you would think. These are hard jobs, and slackers have a hard time sticking in them. It just requires too much work. But every once in a while, you will run into a bad apple and it can really trip you up.

My experience with these people is that they are really good bullshit artists. They will stand and look you in the eye and tell you how much they care about your kid and how much they personally are going to do for your kid. It all looks good, but nothing happens. These people tend to be really good at CYA (cover your ass) strategies and work really hard to make you feel like it's all in your head or that you are overreacting. Be very careful with these wily buzzards. My favorite thing is to give them a task. Something they said they were going to do but didn't, and give them a deadline. This isn't about catching them red-handed. It's about getting clear in your mind if this person is a poser. If you find that they are a poser, FIRE THEM!

People will tell you that you have no authority to fire people from your child's team. Not really true. You have the right to fire any therapist from your child's team—your ABA provider may not be able to replace them for quite a while—so make sure you have good reason for letting them go. You can have your child moved out of a teacher's classroom. You may have to petition and cite reasons, you may even have to move schools, but it is possible. You can stop services with speech teachers, OTs, school psychologists, and other school professionals whenever you want. Don't make a habit of it. Save it for the really bad apples, but know that you can kick anyone off your kid's team when you really need to.

One more note: when you are lucky enough to have good teachers and therapists in your life, praise them! Reward them! Show them you appreciate them as often as you can.

I know we think that rewarding someone is a gift-giving thing, and it can be…but here's a word to the wise: you could spend a bunch of money and never realize that what you got them isn't really their particular currency. Someone once bought me a very expensive designer bag because they wanted me to FEEL their appreciation. I really appreciated the gesture, but I'm not a designer bag kind of gal; I'm just not. I pretended I was, but if they really wanted to make my day, they would hire a reputable cleaning service to come over and clean my house—you know what I'm saying? That would really make my day!

The point is gifts are personal. Choose wisely. You know what tends to be universal is recognition for a job well done. Especially for people who are in career fields that are about care of others…like teachers and therapists. I mentioned earlier you can write letters of recommendation for teachers and therapists and give them to their superiors with a note asking for them to be placed in their permanent file. It's free, and it is a gift that keeps on giving.

What do I mean? I started doing this years ago at the suggestion of another parent. At the end of the year, I write a letter for anyone who has gone the extra mile for my kid. It could be the school nurse, the English teacher, even the principal. I compliment and thank them in the letter and cite examples of something they did that made a difference. I give them the letter with a note saying I have also given it to the principal and asked for it to go in their permanent file and then I do just that. Great.

I feel good that they were thanked. I feel good that I have not spent money but truly given something useful. Then the magic happens. The teacher thanks me for the letter, usually in tears, and tells me how much it means to them to know their work is meaningful. I had one teacher tell me it was the letter of a lifetime that made him happy he had chosen this field. Nice! But the magic is just beginning. The teachers talk to each other. Suddenly good teachers are excited to have my kid in the classroom. Not to get the letter, but because they know they are appreciated... and maybe a little in the hopes they will get a letter. The cycle only helps my son at school. I ask you, has a Starbucks gift card or a Bed Bath and Beyond soap dispenser ever given your kid a boost? I don't think so.

One more thing. Attend every event at school you can. Not just the one your kids are in either, but especially those. Be present. Teachers notice. My favorite tip is to attend school open house events. Get there early if you can. Spend quality time with your child's teacher and then hightail it over to the teachers in the next grade up. SHOP. Meet the teachers, watch them interact with their students and parents. Check out the assignments that are posted around the room. When you introduce yourself, mention you have a child who will be in their grade next year and say your child's name. Watch their face for any reaction. If they light up and say they know your child, BINGO! If they are lukewarm but clearly have heard of your child, RUN; this is not the teacher for your child. If they genuinely act like they don't know who your child is, they probably aren't currently in the running.

Look, schools will tell you they don't decide which teacher a student will have until two weeks before school, and that might be semi-true. Maybe they don't write it in stone until then, but they start talking about it before the end of the year. You don't want your child to end up with a teacher who is lukewarm if you can possibly help it. The school isn't likely to tell you whom they are considering giving your child to, but if you are savvy, you can figure it out at open house and then go back to your coordinator and just say: "Oh, we were in Ms. Knystk's room, and she seems lovely!"

Plant the seed. If the school knows you will be happy with a teacher and they were already thinking of giving you that teacher, they will forge ahead. Ironically, they don't like it if you request a teacher. Be careful of that. It's a fine line. You can also say, "We were in Mrs. Field's classroom, and I don't think that would be a good fit for our child." You don't have to get specific. Just throw it out there. Nicely. Always nicely.

Say this or something like this to yourself:

There are amazing people who want to help me help my child. I am not alone. We are not alone. I am willing to lean into the arms that are embracing us. I allow myself to feel and express gratitude to the people who support us.

CHAPTER

15

Playdates with Neurotypical Moms

I f you are serious about having your child with ASD make as much progress as possible, they are going to need to have playdates with kids who don't have ASD at some point...lots and lots of them. That is going to mean dealing with the neurotypical moms and, in some cases, the neurotypical dads. It isn't always going to go well, so you are going to need lots of different families to choose from. Many of us are overwhelmed by the prospect of this venture. Arrgh! We have to make nice with people we don't even know and then invite them into our house to watch how non-neurotypical our kids are and then have them think things about us and our kid? Yeah! Sign me up! said no parent of a kid on the spectrum ever. But you have to! This is part of the secret sauce. Your child can get thousands of hours of therapy, but if they can't put it all together on the playground with the little snot who picks his nose and calls other kids weird...you are going to continue to have social skills issues, and the older the child, the bigger the impact of social skills issues on their life. On the flip side, the younger the child when you deal with these issues, the less painful it is for them when they fail.

Truth Alert

A disclaimer before I move on: Every child, every person, fails sometimes at social situations. I'm sure that we can all think back to a painful time when someone shunned us publicly. It hurt. So why are we forcing our kids with ASD to go through this? You don't have to. But you may choose to for the same reason every parent of neurotypical kids does. Because having true friends is one of the greatest gifts in life. It isn't easy to find, but it's worth it when you do. Finding, getting, and keeping friends is hard for everyone and often infinitely harder for individuals on the Autism Spectrum. It requires work and patience on everyone's part. I think it is a worthwhile endeavor, if you don't—skip this chapter.

Identifying Good Playdate Material

If your child is under the age of five, the best playdate partner for them is probably the bossiest girl you can find. You know, the one who has "cruise director" written all over her. She probably has younger siblings; she can never get enough attention; and she's constantly barking out orders.

She's your best bet for a lot of reasons.

1. She's going to tell your kid what to do. This is good for now.

2. Just when your kid does what she wants them to do, she's going to change the rules. Your kid needs practice at this, even if they don't like it. This is going to help make your kid more flexible. Let the bossy girl take the flak.

3. Bossy girl's mom is going to appreciate the fact that you like her kid, because lately the other kids haven't wanted to play with her as much. They complain she's too bossy.

4. Bossy girls are loyal and nurturing. If another kid picks on your kid, bossy girl is going to shut that down like an overnight carnival without a permit.

The Forgotten Kid

When your child is a little older, you want to find a child of the same sex as your child who either has a ton or brothers and sisters at home or a mom who is super busy. Why? You're going to need the kid to be available a lot. If there are other kids at home, the mom is going to be thrilled that they are getting attention someplace else, and if the other mom is super busy, this is free childcare for them.

Some of the best advice I ever got was from a mom who had an older son and had already been though all this. She told me to make my house the funniest house on the block. Her advice was to always have the best snacks and treats, always have the coolest stuff going on. My house may not ever be clean, but everybody knows if you want to have a Nerf battle and get taken to the In-N-Out drive thru afterward, come to my house. Yes, some people call it bribery. I call it classical conditioning. We can argue about what to call it. It works. Most of the time. Some kids aren't going to be nice to our kids no matter what we shower them with. Move on, find another kid.

The worst is when your kid gets along with the other kid, but one or both of the parents is really difficult. If it isn't affecting the kids, try not to let it affect you. If it's affecting your kid, do whatever you have to do to keep your kid away from it. Don't let any adult's bad behavior become a self-esteem issue for your kid. It's not worth it.

Be realistic about play dates. They aren't going to be sunshine, light, and happiness, especially in the beginning. Figure out two things you would like to accomplish in each playdate. Maybe all you are working on today is being able to share without crying! If you're not sure what goals would be good for a playdate, ask your ABA team for suggestions. One or two goals is enough. Also keep the play dates short in the beginning. An hour is fine to start. The neurotypical moms won't like that because it isn't enough time to get anything done. You'll work up to longer play dates. Focus on the things you are working on and reward your kid and the other kid when there is progress. People get all squeamish about this, and I don't know why. Tell the kid who comes to your house, "Thank you for playing so patiently with my child. You're such a good friend, and I'm really glad my child has such a good friend." You will see a good kid beam when you say that. They will walk taller and be happier and more patient when they come back. The kid who doesn't like praise might appreciate a piece of candy or a small toy as a thank you. I'm talking about a dollar store toy or a piece of chocolate. Bribery, conditioning? You say tomato. I say tomahto. It works and everybody is happier—what's there to be squeamish about?

I'll tell you what else: it even works when the kid hasn't been patient. WHAT? Compliment a kid in front of their parents and tell them what a good friend they are and how polite they were. The parent looks stunned and then is nicer to the kid all afternoon. The kid can't wait to come back and actually be nice, so you'll do it again. Am I crazy? Try it and you tell me.

Playdates are important. They change over time. Find what works for you, for your kid, and for the kids you have access to. I wanted my friends' kids to be friends with my kid. I have to be honest that that didn't always work out. There was baggage and ultimately resentments. I expected my friends to tell their kids to be a little flexible, a little tolerant of my kid, if nothing else as a favor to me. Looking back, I don't think that was a realistic expectation. I always felt deflated when my friends' kids didn't go the extra mile to be friends with my kid. But not every kid is built that way. I had better luck with kids whose parents I didn't know. And when a kid didn't work out, there were no hard feelings. We moved on to the next kid. My son got lots of practice at being friends with lots of different kids. That's what our kids need.

Say this or something like this:

I am a good parent. I make opportunities for my child to have friends and to practice being a friend. I am helping my child learn social skills by giving them a safe and fun place to be successful.

CHAPTER
16

The Court of Public Opinion

People are going to say stuff about you and your child. They aren't even going to attempt to be informed before they spout whatever their ill-informed opinions are. They may or may not know about your child's diagnosis before they open their mouths and let their brains fall out. But it's going to happen.

You need to try not to let it stop you from what you are doing. It can be a big distraction, and you know, some days you just aren't going to be able to let it go. It might be something really stupid that someone says on your friend's Facebook page or something that your boss says. It could be something you overhear on the playground or even something your mother says at a family dinner. All of a sudden it gets real clear: these people don't get it. They think they do, but they don't. When you can't help yourself, you are going to wade in and speak some truth. It's not going to go well. It can't. You're trying to explain the color blue to people who are colorblind. But you're going to try. Everyone is going to get upset, and there may even be some tears.

Other times you are going to save your breath and say nothing, but you're going to silently steam for hours and hurl words inside your head like "karma" and "ignorance." There are times when what others say is going to scare you and make you want to take your child and retreat to someplace safe emotionally.

It's very important to have at least a small group of parents from the Autism community that you can go to when these things happen. If there isn't a group where you live and you aren't able to start one yourself, join an online group. There are millions of them; they tend to be free, and they will nod in agreement when you tell them how frustrated you are with people who think they know what you're going through but don't have a clue. Find a group that shares the same interests with you, parents whose kids are like your kid.

As our kids age and make different amounts of progress, it gets harder. You really need to be with like-minded parents then. A parent with a high-functioning teenager who constantly wants to retreat into a video game is going to feel ridiculous complaining to a parent of a child who has no verbal language. The thing is we all need a safe place to go and feel both gratitude and frustration. Give yourself the gift of friendship with other parents who can help protect you from the opinions of those who don't know better.

When you can, remember there was a day and a time we didn't know or comprehend there were parents out there fighting for their children instead of thinking about the next Gymboree class. We used to walk around in blessed ignorance not knowing the reality of having a kid who can't communicate so he bangs his head on the floor. We didn't know. Now we do. Now we have work to do to help our children. I encourage you to put your energy into fighting for your child and not fighting with people who are ignorant. And if the day comes when your child is doing better, then I invite you to wade in with those of us who are lucky enough to have free time to fight ignorance. We will welcome your help then, but first things first.

Say this or something like this to yourself:

I am an amazing parent, and I advocate for my child. I won't be stopped by ignorance and prejudice. I will persist in helping my child. People around me may not understand the important path I walk. I will do it anyway.

CHAPTER
17

To Disclose or Not to Disclose

irst let's talk about whether to disclose a diagnosis to the individual with the diagnosis. This is very personal, and you are entitled to your own opinion. I really don't think anyone should be allowed to tell you what to do on this. I will tell you that almost everyone decides at some point to tell the individual, and it is almost always a relief when it happens. Older teens and adults have reported a feeling of finally understanding themselves once they knew. But when and how to tell someone is deeply individual. There's an entire study that is being done on it called The Elephant in the Room Project.[6] There are no answers, just information.

When the time is right how do you tell your child about their diagnosis?

I think there are a few things to keep in mind.
- Keep it positive.
- Don't attach any stigma to the diagnosis.
- Use words that aren't scary or diminishing.

6. Smith-Demers, A. D. (2018). *The Elephant In The Room: The Lived Experience of Talking to Children with ASD About Their Diagnosis.* (Unpublished doctoral thesis). University of Calgary, Calgary, AB. doi:10.11575/PRISM/32049

- Give examples that are inspirational. There are lots of cool people with ASD you can use as examples.

My husband and I made the choice to never keep my son's diagnosis a secret from him. We used the word "Autism" in our house almost daily, and we took every opportunity to point out role models for him. James Durbin was on *American Idol* right after my son was diagnosed, and we were always pointing out how cool he was and saying things like, "Wow he's such a good singer! He's so talented and he has Autism just like you! Isn't that cool." Years later, we all met James Durbin in person and he was thrilled to hear that he had been one of our first role models.

Our choice would not and should not be everyone's choice. You know your child better than anyone. I have great faith you will know when to tell your child.

Telling Other People

If you thought knowing when to tell your child was hard, guess what? Knowing when and how and who to tell about your child's diagnosis is even harder!

For some parents, knowing how and when to disclose to other people is a daily high-wire act. We are forever balancing. And it changes.

When my son was first diagnosed, I told everyone. If you came within five feet of my child, I would tell you.

My thinking was that something bad could happen if I didn't tell you. I quickly discovered that telling people didn't stop bad stuff from happening and sometimes it actually created it! Good times? Not! So I started to get choosier. Who actually needed to know? The mom at the playground whose kid was throwing sand in my kid's eyes didn't need to know. She just needed her kid to stop. But the doctor checking my son's eyes did need to know so he could closely watch for any developmental delays.

I felt that my son's teachers and everyone who worked with him at school needed to know. It didn't always help—sometimes it made it worse—but it gave me a basis upon which I could give information to people who wanted to learn and be helpful.

Side note: the quickest way to see if your child's teacher is a good teacher? Give them some really good information and then see what they do with it. Maybe an article talking about a new study that shows that kids on the spectrum learn better when visual schedules are posted! Good teachers always get excited about learning. Schlock teachers don't want to read. Voila! You instantly know what you are dealing with.

Over the years as my son has changed, my decision of when to disclose has changed as well. Our current rule is that I don't get to disclose without asking his permission. He almost always says, "Yes," but it is necessary and proper for me to ask. The information is his to disclose. That's not always easy to accept. Until recently, a great deal of how I identified myself was as an "Autism Parent." I recently changed that and started referring to myself as a Parent and, when appropriate, as a Parent of an individual who was diagnosed with Autism as a child. Sometimes it gets dicey if I am not at liberty to disclose this. I recently sat with a parent who spent an hour telling me all about kids on the spectrum. She doesn't have any children on the spectrum, but she had lots of opinions. I sat there and listened, saying very little, biting my tongue mostly. On one occasion I couldn't help myself and corrected her on something that was clearly untrue. But I never divulged that I had been on a sixteen-year journey that revolved around an Autism diagnosis. It wasn't mine to tell in that moment. That is the truth. That is what is respectful. It's a quality problem. One that I am grateful to have.

The biggest question we have asked over the years is: "Is it necessary?" This makes it easier to know when to disclose.

If you find yourself in a place where you don't know whether to disclose, ask yourself, "Is it necessary?" Still not sure? Consider waiting until you are sure.

How to disclose has changed for us too.

When he was first diagnosed, I said he was "Autistic." I hated saying it. Some of my best friends prefer to be called "Autistics." I honor that; I can only tell you what I felt, and it never felt right for me when referring to my son. It felt wrong.

Then I heard Holly Robinson Peete on *Oprah* say "has Autism," and I started saying that. It felt better, but not right. I would say, "My son has Autism."

Then we started therapy, and I wanted to say something positive. For five years, we said, "He is actively recovering from Autism." It made people crazy, but it felt good to say. People had/have very strong reactions to "r" words. We will come back to the word "recovery" later. If this is hard for you, remember to breathe.

Then we started saying "was diagnosed with Autism as a child" or "was given an Autism Spectrum Diagnosis."

I usually avoided saying "disorder" or "disability". It doesn't fit my son. There was a time when it did. It doesn't anymore.

I say "high-functioning" when I know that I am talking to people who won't understand other words. I hate it when I have to say that. But it is me "dumbing down" the conversation for ignorance's sake. The term "high-functioning" is so subjective, and it requires context. All of us have things we are better at than other things. But we don't walk around saying things like, "I'm high-functioning because I can do my own taxes." What does "high-functioning" even mean? I used to think it meant the person was able to speak. I have since met so many amazing individuals who use assistive technology to communicate who have more ability than I ever hope to have.

What you say has to serve two functions: it has to communicate what you want to communicate, and it has to be something you can feel good about. This is your child you are talking about.

Don't be afraid to try out what works for you and change it when it no longer works. When and if it is appropriate, allow your child to tell you what they think. Don't be surprised when they change their minds. This, too, is a quality problem.

The current language my son prefers is "was diagnosed with Autism as a child." This is what is accurate for him. It is only my job to listen.

Words matter—we will delve further into the muck of words and labels later.

Note: Since writing this book I have started referring to myself as a PONI (pronounced PONY) Which stands for Parent of a Neurodiverse Individual and sometimes even a PONAI, Parent of a Neurodiverse Adult Individual. This is what my son and I are comfortable with now.

CHAPTER
18
Teenage Years

Big Fat Disclaimer: I'm still figuring this one out. My son is nineteen. I spent years asking the experts questions to be as prepared as possible, and I have managed so far, but I am still in the trenches on this. So here are my current thoughts. Check back with me in a couple of years to see if it worked!

1. *Feed their passion.* According to Temple Grandin, this is one of the most important things you can do. But don't be linear in your thinking on this. If your kid likes video games, make them learn how they are made and get them to create their own game. Don't just let them play!

2. *Make them work and volunteer.* Everyone agrees that adults with ASD are underemployed. The teen years are a great time to give them experience in employment with paper routes, mowing lawns, doing chores, volunteering to help charities, etc. Make sure you are teaching and modeling good work ethics: showing up on time, doing your best, etc.

Note: This has really paid off, and I have to give props to the late great Joanne Lara. She never let a day go by without reminding me that ALL our kids need to work; work means a seat at the table. She jammed this down my throat, and I listened. I now have a kid who LOVES to work! See Joanne's book in the reference at the end of the chapter.

3. *Give well-defined rules.* Everything gets a little grayer in the teen years, not just the parents. Our kids have been taught rules that don't seem to be enforced in other kid's behaviors. We teach them to be nice to people, but sometimes the rudest, meanest kid is the most popular at school. What's up with that? Teen years are a great time to redefine the rules of what is important and why it's important to us, even if it's not important to others. As much as possible, give them meaningful rewards for following the rules.

4. *Build good friendships.* Now more than ever is the time to make your house be the place the kids hang out. It ensures your kid has friends, and it means that you will know what is going on. Chances are your kid won't tell you the dirt, but their talkative friend who loves donuts will! Have the parties at your house. Let them make a mess. You can always clean up a messy house. It's worth it to know what

is going on in your kid's life and to cement in good friends.

5. *Think about what behaviors you want to reinforce.* Make sure you are giving huge rewards for studying (even if it doesn't translate to great grades), telling the truth (even when, especially when, it's something that isn't good), and doing what you said you were going to do. Too often parents forget what the long-term goals are and reinforce things that don't lead to good adult habits. Or worse, we punish things that we really shouldn't or that send a mixed message. For instance, we tell our kids to tell us the truth, they tell us something, and we punish them. What's more important to you? That your child tells you things or that you punish them when they do something wrong? There is no hard and fast answer for all scenarios, but I try to reward my son when he tells me something. So in my house you don't get punished if you tell the truth. You might get a lecture, but I actually reward the telling of the truth. Judge me. I'm okay with it. Guess why? Your opinion of my parenting is none of my business!

6. *Tell them you love them and that you are proud of them more than you think is necessary.* They stop getting their self-esteem from us sometime in the teen years

and start getting it from their peers, but keep filling that bucket any time you can. It can't hurt.

7. *Accept them for who they are, and love them for that.* This is a critical time for a parent and child. Being a teenager does not mean you are fully solidified in who you are, but you can get a pretty good picture of who someone is. It's time to see them, clearly, for who they are and accept them that way. She doesn't have vocal speech? It's time to set the grief aside and accept that. It doesn't mean she can't continue to grow; it means loving her where she is. He doesn't like basketball and that was the dream you had for him? It's time to dream a new dream. Go back to the grief chapter. Work it out. But know that is your work. It has nothing to do with your child. Don't miss out on knowing this amazing person because you got caught up in who you thought they would be.

Truth Alert

This is something all parents need to do, regardless of whether their kid is on the spectrum. Did your parent do this for you? Do you remember how good it felt? Give this gift to your child. They will feel the shift even if they don't fully understand it. If your parent didn't give this gift to you, ask yourself what it would have meant to you to have your parent fully accept and appreciate you for who you are. It's big, right? Do this for your child.

8. *Don't stop seeking progress, but get more specific.* You're tired, your kid is tired. You've accepted them for who they are—so we're done, right? NO. All human beings continue to grow, every day. We get better at things, or we lose skills from not maintaining them...all of us. So don't make the mistake of giving up in the teen years; just get more specific. Pick the things you really need them to work on and the things they really want to work on and get serious about those things. One little asterisk here: your teen may let you know they want to work on something that requires a prerequisite skill. Make sure they understand how the prerequisite skill will help them reach their goal. This can be as simple as a First-Then visual schedule. But take the time to explain it. You will have better compliance if they understand this is working toward their goal. It is normal for teenagers to be oblivious to the hard work and steps required to achieve their dreams; part of our job is to help them through this phase. Sally might say that she wants to be a veterinarian. She may really mean she wants to work with animals. Either way, we should begin giving her ways

to figure it out, while helping her to know that there are many steps to becoming a veterinarian. You have to be good at math to be an animal doctor; does Sally like math? There's really no limit to what can be done to help Sally with her dream. We can introduce her to real veterinarians. Maybe there is a volunteer job at the local shelter. There are books, videos, TV shows, and even movies that might help Sally see vets on the job. It's so important to give our teens the "full picture."

9. *Get help when you need it.* Anxiety, depression, and suicidal thoughts are prevalent in teens on the spectrum. Watch your teens closely.

   Insurance now pays for ABA and CBT for teens. Don't listen to those who say there is no help for teens. There are also social groups and teen services springing up all over the country. Seek help whenever you need it. Don't take the mindset that things will just work themselves out when they "grow out of it."

10. *If you have to have your teen leave your home…* This is a hard one. Everyone, breathe. Sometimes, being in your home is not what is best for your child. Breathe.

    There are lots of reasons why a child should not remain in your care in your home. Here are just some of the reasons.

- *Your child is a danger to themselves or others.*

  If you or anyone is in danger, it's time to face facts and get everyone safe. This is unimaginably hard, but it is easier than having to deal with the aftermath if it isn't dealt with. A proper facility can help your child to work on whatever is causing them to hurt themselves or others. Do your research and make sure your child is going to a reputable facility where there are no aversive strategies employed. Stay in contact with the facility and your child. Ask to learn everything about what they are doing with your child so you can uphold it when you visit or when they visit you.

- *No one in the house is physically capable of taking care of the individual.*

  When your child was three, you could physically pick them up and put them into the bathtub. Now they are thirty-seven and you are sixty-three. The equation no longer works. If they aren't capable of taking care of themselves and you can't do it either, then who can? If there is no one, it is time to look at an assisted living facility. I cannot stress how important it is to do this well before it becomes a necessity. Many individuals find they enjoy living in an assisted living situation or a group home. It's social, there are friends to converse with, and there are often more activities available to them. When a healthy parent places their child in one of these well-researched facilities (do your homework!) there is an easy transition. The parent comes to visit, the individual may come home for the holidays, everything is smooth. They become used to their new home and feel comforted by being there.

If the transition to this situation happens because the parent is sick or has died, the transition is accompanied by grief and fear. It's a much harder transition. Please consider placing your child while both of you are healthy and you can monitor if the facility is truly the best place for your child.

- *You aren't mentally capable of taking care of your child.*

There is no way to candy-coat this one. It is natural for parents of special needs kids to sometimes feel overwhelmed and even have doubts about whether they can handle everything that is thrown at them. It's normal. Talking to others who are going through it can be very helpful. What isn't normal is when a parent begins to feel their child can only be safe with them. This kind of thinking requires professional help. We have seen too often what happens when a parent feels the child is only safe with them and they aren't able to continue taking care of the child. It is unthinkable. In this heightened state of psychosis, parents have harmed their children and even murdered their children, all while saying they were trying to keep their children safe. If you find yourself feeling like you are the only one who can take care of your child, seek help immediately. If you are having thoughts of harming yourself or your child, call 911. Please read Chapter 24 ("If You Can't Go On") for more information.

It takes a brave parent to admit they are not up to taking care of their child. It may conjure feelings of failure. Giving your child to the care of someone else when you aren't able to take care of them is truly loving your child. I have seen many parents need to take a break and then be able to have their children live with them later. I have seen other parents discover their children are happier living with someone else. It doesn't have to be a negative thing to have your child leave your home. This is usually the goal with neurotypical children! It is important not to stigmatize this transition for individuals on the spectrum.

Say this or something like this:

It is the natural order of things to have my child live somewhere else at some point. I choose to support my child by giving them the opportunity to live elsewhere so they can grow and be their best self. I will allow myself the freedom to be my child's parent no matter where they live. I do this for myself and my child.

Resources

Baker, Jed. *Overcoming Anxiety in Children and Teens*. Arlington, TX: Future Horizons, Inc., 2015.

Lara, Joanne, and Susan Osborne. *Teaching Pre-Employment Skills to 14–17 Year-Olds: The Autism Works Now!® Method*. London: Jessica Kingsley Publishers, 2017.

Grandin, Temple. *Calling All Minds: How to Think and Create like an Inventor*. New York, NY: Puffin Books, 2019.

CHAPTER 19

Self-Advocates

Self-Advocates in the Autism Community are adults who are on the Autism Spectrum themselves.

I love this group of people, but they don't always love me. I frequently find that I have the potential to offend and annoy members of this community.

Let me be clear that I respect, admire, and support these individuals and their right to tell me and others when we have offended them. It is never my purpose to offend, but when I do and they tell me off, I first try to correct myself, but I have to be honest. I silently celebrate and think to myself, "Good for you! You have the ability to tell me your opinion! And stand up for your rights! Right on." Oh, and when appropriate, I apologize, but that I do out loud.

Sometimes I apologize for offending, but I keep doing what I am doing. I have to keep talking about therapies I believe in. I believe in good-quality ABA. I watched five years of it in my home. It's not an urban myth. I would never allow my kid to be mistreated. I shudder when I think, what if I had been talked out of doing ABA forever? There are people, especially children in the Autism community, who do not have the ability to speak for themselves, even with the assistance of technology. We as parents are their voice. We have a responsibility to speak on their behalf. So I continue to speak on behalf of good-quality, mindful ABA.

There are self-advocates who tell me they are opposed to ABA therapy because it requires the child to behave in a way that the child doesn't want to behave. They believe it changes who the child would be. That is not acceptable to them, and they will often define it as being torturous. They will say this to new parents in an attempt to dissuade them from doing ABA with their small children. These self-advocates will point to themselves as examples. Some of them had ABA therapy many years ago; some did not. They have told me that they are fine, exactly the way they are. I agree with them. But sometimes they have skills our children don't have. They are capable of telling us their thoughts and feelings. Is there a parent out there who would not be thrilled to have this kind of a conversation with their kid who is on the spectrum? No! We would light our hair on fire and dance in the street to be able to have this level of discussion with our kids! We HOPE that our kids grow up and have opinions and the ability to say, "That hurts my feeling when you say that!" We HOPE they will have the ability to go online and post a comment that says, "When you say that it infringes upon my rights as a person and suggests that my way of thinking is wrong, just because it isn't your way of thinking!" Can I get an AMEN?? That is what we're working for. And it takes work, work I believe we owe it to our kids to help them to do.

Welcome self-advocates into your life. Encourage them to speak their minds. Learn from them about what we do that is ableist and inappropriate. Try not to take it personally when you get it wrong; we all have room to grow in this area. But make a place in your life for adults on the spectrum. Love them for who they are and the example they set for our kids. They are AWESOME. Just don't let them talk you out of doing good, quality therapy with your kid. I respect their opinions and their experiences with old and poor-quality ABA. I champion their cause to stamp that out. I stand with them on this. We need to end practices that are punitive and harmful to individuals. Of course! But I do not believe they are talking about the practices of good-quality ABA, which is individual-specific and requires that the teaching be meaningful to the individual. If there is a self-advocate who reads this and disagrees, please write to me and I will be happy to arrange for you to view really good ABA therapy, the stuff that is helping more and more of our kids be more and more like you. Please, take me up on my offer. I'm 100 percent confident that good-quality

ABA empowers children, and I'd be happy to show you that.

For parents, spend time with adults on the spectrum whenever you can. It's a great way to look into the future and be filled with hope and pride. More importantly, you will meet remarkable people who will enrich your life just through knowing them. I have certainly found this to be true. Years ago, I can remember being so excited to meet an adult on the spectrum and to hear them talk about their life! It was amazing. I don't know when I realized that most of the people whose company I enjoy the most are individuals on the spectrum, but it's true.

Whatever we do, we must always uphold the rights of individuals to tell their own stories when, how, and where they choose to.

Say this or something like this:

I am grateful for the self-advocates in my life. I am enriched by hearing their voices and by listening to their wisdom. They are showing me a future with my child and all its possibilities.

CHAPTER
20

Cancer, Eviction,
Fires & Floods

I used to believe if you were dealt an "Autism card" that it meant the Universe would take it easy on you with everything else. It is laughable how naive that thought was. I pictured this giant boardroom where God made decisions. And anytime they would be doling out challenges around the world, God would raise his benevolent hand from time to time, causing everyone to pause, and he would say, "You can't visit that upon them. We already gave them a child on the Autism spectrum." Everyone in the room would knowingly, solemnly nod in agreement and get back to work finding someone else to visit challenges upon, because clearly that family had enough to deal with. Ha! Like a child, I was so disappointed when I found out how many Autism parents end up being diagnosed with Cancer (it's higher than the normal Cancer rate!) Autism doesn't give you a pass. Autism families get evicted—happened to my family twice in the years we were doing therapy. They get diagnosed with Cancer and other diseases. They experience floods, fires, tornadoes, and tsunamis just like everyone else. Spouses die, car accidents happen... it isn't bad luck, it's life. And if you find yourself thinking that you have it bad, look around; I'm 100 percent sure that someone has it worse than you.

I often refrain from telling people about some of the ridiculous stuff that happened to us—because it starts to sound ridiculous. At one point our landlord had died, but his ex-wife didn't tell us. There may have been some shady business, where someone might have been cashing rent checks they weren't entitled to and that weren't going to the bank to pay the mortgage on the property. Maybe. Eventually a bank person showed up at our door and informed us that we were now squatters. Surprise! Just what you always hoped you would grow up to be! We couldn't leave because we couldn't get our deposit back, and as luck would have it, the air conditioning and the dryer quit almost simultaneously! It was August in southern California. Temperatures in the triple digits. So I did the only thing I could. During the day, I washed our clothes, while my son had therapy in our house, which grew hotter by the hour. In the evening, as the last therapist left, my husband and I would hang an elaborate system of clotheslines throughout the house and hang the wet clothing from every inch of it. The clothes would dry while lowering the temperature to a bearable level so we could sleep and start over again the next morning. We did that for months while we looked for another place to move. We cooperated with the bank that now owned the condo, and when we could, we moved.

Looking back, it seems like someone else's life. I didn't think too much about the heat or the clothesline because I was in constant fear that we would be homeless. It was close. I know many families that became homeless after their children were diagnosed with Autism. It happens, often through no fault of the family. We had been paying our rent—who plans on their landlord dying? The point is stuff happens. To everybody. Autism doesn't stop that and can often make it worse. The good news? You have a community to go to if it does happen to you. Almost every Autism organization has a fund or an emergency protocol for when bad stuff happens to families dealing with Autism. You have to ask for help and be diligent. Help doesn't always come the first time you ask, and it frequently doesn't show up on the timetable that you truly need it.

Keep asking for help and be willing to help people help you. Tell people what you need, but be willing to compromise. It's hard. When we asked for help in finding a place to live, people came out of the woodwork trying to help us, but we were insistent that we had to live in our son's current school district. We weren't trying to be difficult;

we had an IEP in place with a 1:1 aide who was trained, and we loved her. If we moved to another school district. we knew we were going to lose that. As we were preparing to move to a hotel, the school district heard what was happening. We were literally going to become homeless to comply with their rules, and they relented. They allowed us to take a temporary apartment in a nearby area with the understanding that it was just for that school year. By the new school year, we would have to be in district, or we were out.

As luck would have it, the new landlord lost his condo to foreclosure, we were once again evicted, and with only days to spare we moved into an apartment in my son's school district. It was a horrible, cockroach-infested nightmare. We lasted eleven months there before we could get out. My skin crawls every time I think of it. But we survived that and worse. You can too. Speak up, ask for help. Put your shoulders back and keep working. Take the problems one at a time. It does improve.

Things to remember:

1. Prioritize health. Death is the only thing you can't bounce back from. Don't put off tests and procedures that help you stay healthy.

2. Do what you have to do to keep a roof over your head, even if it isn't yours and it isn't perfect.

3. Remember to be grateful for what you have instead

of focusing on what you don't have. Things can usually get worse, so be grateful.

4. When you feel like you are in a poop storm, ask for help and keep asking. Keep working and keep asking. Accept help when it shows up.

Say this or something like this:

Today I will focus on survival and I will remember to breathe. I will put one foot in front of the other and do what is necessary to survive. I will hold hope in my heart that a day is coming when we will once again survive and thrive... Until then, I will breathe.

People to Ask for Help

Autism Care Today!

http://www.act-today.org/ *(Ask about an SOS grant.)*

Autism Speaks

https://www.autismspeaks.org/financial-autism-support (This is a comprehensive list of resources to help with all financial needs, including rent.)

TACA Parent Support Network

www.tacanow.org

Families for Early Autism Treatment (FEAT)

http://www.feat.org/

Autism Society of America

www.autism-society.org

Council of Parent Attorneys and Advocates

www.copaa.org

Doug Flutie Foundation

https://www.flutiefoundation.org/apply-grant

CHAPTER
21
Gratitude &
Farting Rainbows

By now you have probably heard some parent proudly proclaim that they are so grateful for Autism, that they now realize it is a blessing, and their life is better for having had a child with Autism... and you might be thinking to yourself: "What the BLEEP?" Are these folks for real? Maybe. Let me explain.

As far as I can tell, there are five stages to the acceptance of being a Parent of an individual on the Autism Spectrum.

1. **The River in Egypt—Denial**

   Everybody goes through this stage at some point, and many people hang out here an extended period of time. This is the phase where you are convinced that there is nothing wrong with your child. You become angry when people point out things that your child can't or doesn't do that other kids can do. You are furious that your child is being judged by some arbitrary schedule that says kids talk by a certain age or fit in by a certain age. Who makes up these rules anyway? Do they take individuality into consideration? If everybody would just leave your kid alone, he/she would probably be just fine.

The tough thing about denial is that eventually you see that with help your child could do more, and you can't argue that they need help and they don't need help at the same time...It gets dicey, so one or both parents move on to...

2. **Super Hero Mode**

This is where one or both of the parents decides they are going to do everything humanly possible to help their child. Some parents will be drawn to the biomedical side of things and focus intently on diet and supplements; others will learn the principals of ABA and practice them twenty-four hours a day. Others will start equine therapy and rent HBOT time. Everyone will do research and then try to follow through, clinging to hope. Some parents will do everything, frantic, hoping they didn't miss something.

The super hero mode lasts as long as the child keeps making progress, until the funding runs out or one or both of the parents breaks mentally or physically.

Then comes...

3. **Depression**

Depression is inevitable and can come at any time. People think that it only comes to parents whose kids don't make a lot of progress. Nothing could be further from the truth. I always warn parents of kids who do so well that they no longer need therapy to be on the lookout for a crushing depression; it's usually coming. Depression comes in all sizes and shapes. It comes when people don't know how to survive when not in crisis mode. It comes when you realize that "this" might be as good as it gets. It comes when you realize that Autism is not going to take a vacation. It comes when you realize this is your life. It's important to talk about depression and to get help. Unchecked, Depression can lead to ...

4. **Stagnation and cynicism**

This is the phase where everything gets numb. It just hurts too much to feel anymore. If you allow yourself to feel anything, it's blame. Blame for anyone who said they could help your kid and didn't, blame for yourself because maybe you did something wrong and that's why your kid didn't make as much progress. Yeah, this is the space where we compare what other people have and wonder why they got so lucky. We get stuck here and can't get out. People make suggestions, and it all seems ridiculous and overwhelming. Besides which, we've tried everything already! What's the point?

The only way out of this phase is to mix a healthy dose of hope with action.

And lastly, occasionally there is...

5. Acceptance.

Acceptance is when you stop wondering who your kid would be if it weren't for Autism, and you just see them. This is who they are. This isn't something that comes in the early days. It can't fully. But there can be glimmers. Your child does something that is uniquely them. In the beginning you might even ask yourself, Is that the Autism or is that them? With time, in a bittersweet way, those thoughts fade. Your child is your child, they are interchangeable with their experiences. For a lot of parents I know, this crossroad seems to appear from the ages of ten to sixteen. Somewhere in there, you begin to get a sense of what you are "left with." For some there is the crushing blow that despite their best efforts, their child is likely never going to live independently. This is devastating and not to be taken lightly. There is a grieving process that is necessary to let go of the hopes and expectations of what their life was supposed to be like. But there is something extraordinary that happens when someone allows themselves the grief of what is not meant to be. It often makes room for the notion of what can be. This is also acceptance. Okay, he isn't going to live independently, so where is he going to live, especially when I am gone? Tough stuff, but once it has been surmounted, there is peace and true happiness. Acceptance isn't an arrival destination. It is a state of mind that ebbs and flows and is supplanted by the four other stages and then returns.

Acceptance does not mean contentment. It doesn't mean that you start farting rainbows with puzzle pieces on them and every moment is an endless swirl of joy. Nope. Not even close. But acceptance allows you to be in Gratitude for what you do have. I remember a Dad explaining to me that "He didn't find his voice until his child didn't have one." That's acceptance; that is gratitude. No farted rainbows, no expectation of perfection. In fact, there is some pretty stark reality implied there, but it is beautiful. Can you get to acceptance? Yes. Give it time, and don't allow yourself to get stuck in any of the other phases.

Say this or something like this:

Today, I will find something to be grateful for, and I will choose to focus on that. It may be something small, but I will be grateful. I will think about all I have and not focus on what I don't have. I will not compare myself or my child to anyone else. I will appreciate what is and let the rest go so I can be in this moment.

CHAPTER
22

Finding Your Niche

Everybody has a role to play in the Autism community. You don't have to look far to find yours. What interests you? What are you drawn to? What keeps showing up in your life? The first thing that interested me about Autism was diet. I am allergic to wheat; I break out into hives and get very hot, angry and uncomfortable when I have wheat. I can't concentrate. It made sense to me that wheat might have an effect on how my child learned. So early on, I became very interested in diet.

I was NOT interested in ABA. I had promised our developmental pediatrician that I was not going to do ABA and I meant it. But ABA kept getting in my face. It would not leave me alone. The universe, thank GOD, all but tied me to a chair and said, "Do this." When I saw how well ABA worked with my son, I just had to know more and more and more.

When my son was in preschool, I met a mom who was obsessed with all of the biomedical and chemical info. It hurt my head to think of it. We even went to an Autism

Research Institute conference together, and I remember saying that if one more person showed me a slide of a peptide of gluten or casein, I was going to run screaming from the building with my hair on fire. My biomedical mom was in heaven.

A few years later, I went to an ABAI conference to interview several of the speakers. My camerawoman threatened to quit after I did fifty-two interviews in just over two days. I wasn't even aware of the fact we were working! I was fascinated and engaged and wanted to know more. When you find something that interests you, you will find time just flies!

So what interests you? What do you want to know more about? You don't have to limit your interests to one area, but follow your passions. If something intrigues you, chase it down. Call the place that is doing the research, and ask questions. The Autism community is wide open; there is nobody who is unreachable. The first book I read that made a huge difference to me was Christina Adam's *A Real Boy*. It was my bible in the first year. I couldn't imagine then that I would ever meet her, and now I consider her a friend. My shoes have sat under her kitchen table! My kid has left stuff in her refrigerator! How cool is that?

You want to meet Temple Grandin? You can! Go to one of her talks! She does book signings! Make it happen.

There's room for you at the table; all you have to do is take the seat that appeals to you. So get involved when you're ready. We need you.

Say this or something like this:

I am a valued and valuable member of the Autism Community. I have unique talents and interests to bring to the table. I am excited to help others on this journey.

CHAPTER

23

Giving Back

When you first become a member of the Autism Community, your to-do list is long and cumbersome. In the first year, you really need to focus on your kid and your family and getting the help and support you need to survive and thrive. It's good to connect to the community as soon as you can so you can get information and get support. Your focus in the early days should not be about giving back. You can't give away what you don't have—so first things first—take care of your family and get yourself on track.

You will start to know when it is your turn to give back. It will start small. Someone will ask you a question and you will answer it. At first you may not feel qualified, but then you realize how much you have learned and how much that can help other people. Shortly after that, you will have an opportunity to volunteer. There are sooooo many ways to volunteer and so many organizations to choose from. You may already have an idea to start your own organization! This is great, but go help someone else first. You need that training before you are ready to start your own movement. Help organizations that helped you or that you wish you'd known about. Do things that help you see a difference but that don't prevent you from doing what your family needs. Never lose sight of what your kid needs. That still comes first. Sometimes people will come to me with ideas for Autism Live that would have me traveling the globe and never being at home for my kid. Not going to happen. I have limits. I have priorities. But I give back every day. It is important to pay it forward. Giving back is the best thing I know to ward off depression and keep hope alive. Give back as much as you can, but not at the sacrifice of your family.

Say this or something like this:

I am grateful for all I have learned and all the support I have received. I am excited that I now have something to give back. I have the ability to help others and I am willing to share what I know.

CHAPTER
24

When You Can't Go On

First of all, let's leave judgments at the door. I don't know a single Autism parent who hasn't, at least once, wondered if they were going to be able to go on. This is not an easy gig. It can be a big, fat, hairy, scary test that you don't feel up to. Join the club. Feeling fearful and overwhelmed doesn't make you a bad parent. It makes you human. But if you think I'm going to tell you to just suck it up and go on, guess again. No, I'm going to ask you to do something much scarier. I'm going to ask you to be honest with someone and get help. Yeah, that's the harder choice. It means you have to trust someone, and sometimes that doesn't work out. But you have to try... it's best to try before things get really dire, but that isn't always possible. Many parents are eligible for respite, which is when someone is paid to be with your child so you can have a break. Many funding sources pay for this because they know it is essential for good mental health. The problem is it takes a lot of work to set it up and get it started, and if you're already going down the tubes, it can be just too overwhelming.

If that is you, you need to pick the person you trust the most in life and tell them "I need you to watch my child" and if possible, transport your child to them. Then do the one thing you need to do the most while your child is there. For a lot of people, that would be sleep. Sleep in your car outside the house where you left your child if that's what it takes. For some people, you might need to use that time to call other people and ask for help. Call your local health and human resources office, call the organizations listed in the back of the book. Call a first responder if there is an imminent emergency. Call everyone you know until you get help.

TRUTH ALERT

You might not like the help you get. You might not like it for yourself or your child, but sometimes things have to come to an ugly stop in order to get better.

BIG TRUTH ALERT

There is a horrible but documented phenomena among caretakers where when they get to a place where they feel they have no choice, they decide to take not only their own life, but also the life of their child. This is not acceptable, and when we are mentally right, none of us would argue differently. But things get confused when people are not mentally right. PLEASE, before you get there, have the courage to ask for help and take it. We have seen the parents who were not able to get or take help, who felt so stuck they took their own children's lives. There is no help for those parents now. There is no peace for them ever. Promise yourself that you will ask for help when you need it. For your sake, for your child's sake, do this.

Say this or something like this:

I can always ask for help. There are wonderful people who want to help me and won't judge me if I ask for help. Asking for help is the most loving thing I can do for my child.

CHAPTER
25

Language & Functional Communication

I have yet to meet an Autism parent who doesn't wish for verbal speech for their child. We all want our kids to be able to talk. The good news is that more kids with ASD are able to talk than ever before. In the 80s, if an individual was diagnosed with Autism, there was an assumption they would never have functional speech. Early intensive behavioral intervention has flipped this script, and more and more children are speaking. While this is great news, there is still a percentage of children who, despite intensive therapies, won't achieve verbal speech. It is essential, critical, mandatory that we give all individuals the empowerment of functional communication.

Every person on the planet has a right to be able to communicate their basic needs, and if it is not given to a person, no one within the immediate vicinity of that person will be happy or comfortable.

Think about it. If you were taken hostage by a group of aliens and you did not know their mode of communication, how long would it take for you to resort to violent behavior? Would it be after two hours of trying to get a drink of water? Or would it be when you needed to use the restroom? I'm pretty sure it would take about fifteen minutes before I would get really nasty. I would need something, water, a sweater, a fan, a mint...something, and if I couldn't communicate that need, things would start to go downhill. I'm an adult who understands when and why my body is uncomfortable, but I would start throwing things if I couldn't be understood by the people around me. I would bite, kick, pull people's hair. I might even throw my own poo if you didn't let me use the toilet when I wanted to. Why not? What would I have to lose?

What must it be like for a child with ASD? The frustration has to be enormous. For children who do not have spoken language, we have a responsibility to give them some means of communication. We call this functional communication. It could be a Picture Exchange System (PECs) or other Iconic Communication, it could utilize technology, or it could involve sign language. Different styles for different individuals. It takes a while to teach functional communication and it can be frustrating for the learner, but it is sooooo worth it.

I always think of how long it took Annie Sullivan to get Helen Keller to understand that the motions she was making with her hand meant water. It practically killed everyone in the household, but finally Helen got it, and then she understood "doll," and although there was probably more frustration down the road, the majority of what came afterwards was just miraculous. Helen's life began. She could communicate. She could learn and teach. We need to be like Annie Sullivan and not give up when the going gets tough.

I think the hardest part for parents is feeling the disappointment of giving up on speech. That is the reality of what it feels like when a therapy team suggests that a child learn functional communication. "They're giving up. They don't think my child will ever speak. I'm not giving up on my child!" That's what it feels like. That's not what it is. Remember in the beginning of this chapter, it used to be the presumption was our kids wouldn't talk, and now the majority of them do have verbal communication... what changed? One of the things we know for sure is that a child who is not speaking is more likely to learn to speak if they learn functional communication first than if they don't. Wait... What? If your child is not learning to speak, on their own or after a few months of intensive, quality ABA therapy...they are more likely to learn to speak if you teach them functional communication first. So if the team says it's time to shift to functional communication, get excited. Get on board! You will see that there are some intense rewards.

When children have functional communication, tantrums and other challenging behavior diminishes. It takes a lot of energy to throw a fit. I'll do it if I have to, if that's really what it takes to get what I want. But if I don't have to. If I can point to a glass of juice and you'll give it to me, I don't need to throw a fit. It makes sense. Give your children the gift of communication, whatever it takes.

Don't believe me? Ask someone who uses assistive technology if you should wait to give your child functional communication. Then stand back because they are going to furiously type words, some of which aren't going to be pretty. They'll get you motivated.

One more important note. Whatever means you give your child for functional communication, they should be given access to it at all times. All the time. There are no excuses. You can never take their device away as a punishment or decide to leave it at home. I think most people get this, but for some reason it gets a little sketchy in the real world. It's raining out, so the teacher puts the device in the student's backpack before putting them on the bus. Ummm. No. Do we take away the other student's abilities to communicate when it's raining? No. So we can't do it for this student. Instead we invest in a protective covering and/or insure the device. Often I will hear a parent say they had to limit the child's access to their iPad because they were spending too much time playing games. If the iPad is the child's means of communication, this won't work. Instead parents can change the settings on the device. They can specify what programs can be accessed so the child has access to their communication apps but not games. It is important to militantly protect your child's access to their means of functional communication. I always think of Ursula, the sea witch in *The Little Mermaid*. She took Ariel's voice. She was a villain. Don't be Ursula. Don't let anyone around your child be Ursula.

Say this or something like this:

My child has the right to communicate at all times, and I choose to listen to all forms of communication. Communicating with my child is one of my highest priorities.

CHAPTER
26

R words: Retarded, Recovery, Remission, Resentment

Words have meaning. They can start a war, heal a tired soul, and make someone grateful to be alive. They can stop you in your tracks or spur you on to do something you once thought was impossible. Words can hurt our feelings or the feelings of people we love. Autism is surrounded by words that carry a lot of weight, none more so than a group of words that start with the letter R.

We are all too familiar with the dreaded "R" word: Retarded. Thanks to a PR campaign, it is widely understood now that Retard and Retarded are unacceptable words to use in conjunction with anyone, but especially individuals with developmental delays. The trouble is until very recently it was still a legal medical distinction to be dubbed Mentally Retarded (MR). The stigma attached to the words is overwhelming, but for the purposes of this book, I feel like it is important to note that even in cases where MR is still diagnosed, neither MR nor the newer term, Intellectual Disability (ID), is the same thing as ASD. The vast majority of individuals with ASD do not qualify for a diagnosis of MR or ID, and for those that do, it is said to be "comorbid." This simply means the two things are different, but in this individual they exist together. It does not mean they are the same or they always exist together. It would be the same as saying that all people with Cancer are also bipolar. They aren't, although you can be bipolar and have cancer; it does occur in some cases, but not always.

Another controversial word in the field of Autism is "Recovery." There are people who use the word "recovery" when a person who has a qualified diagnosis makes such significant progress that they no longer meet the criteria for a diagnosis of Autism Spectrum Disorder. It doesn't mean that the person's brain has changed or that they no longer have any difficulties. It does mean that they no longer require support to be able to live their lives to the fullest.

People get so emotional about the word Recovery. I have had self-advocates tell me that it diminishes them, offends them, and tells them that they are something to be cured of. I will tell you honestly that it does not make me feel that. It makes me feel hopeful for a new generation of young people who will bring their unique brains to the world's problems and find solutions that the rest of us can't imagine. And maybe they won't have to go through debilitating anxiety to be able to do it. That sounds thrilling to me. But I have all but stopped using the word "recovery" because of my friends who tell me it hurts them. I have not stopped talking about the concept of recovery, though; I believe in it. I have seen it with my own eyes; I know it is possible to make so much progress that the disabling aspects of Autism are overcome while the differences remain.

I feel the need to make clear: this is NOT about trying to CURE Autism or to make Autism non-existent. In my opinion, this is about reducing and removing challenges so you can allow the individual to shine. Maybe "recovery" isn't the right word; maybe we need to create a new word. A word that describes being different but not disabled. I will tell anyone who will listen that my son's brain is BETTER than mine. It's sharper, more elegant. It sees around corners and can foresee problems in a way that my brain can't. Why would anyone want to change or diminish that? But what a crying shame it would have been if my son had never been able to communicate his thoughts? What a loss! I can't even bear to think of it. Now imagine it's not just one individual. Imagine two percent of our population not able to share their wisdom; it's soul-crushing. I don't want to change those individuals; I want to support them in finding a way to overcome what is in their way.

Now with quality ABA more prevalent, there are more and more children with an ASD diagnosis who are reaching the state where they cannot be described as being disabled. Insurance companies need a way to code that for their records. They have settled on the word "Remission." New "R" word; just as much controversy! One parent whose child was deemed "in remission from Autism" told me the doctor had expressed that her child, who had previously qualified for a diagnosis of a disorder, now didn't qualify for the disorder, but he couldn't be sure that wouldn't change one day … thus remission.

I encourage you to make your own decisions on the words you use and don't use in your life to describe how you feel about yourself. I invite you to honor how others choose to utilize words to describe themselves. It sort of makes me bonkers when someone tells me or my son what words we should use. I hope I haven't made you feel that way in any point of this book. I think we might need a new word here too.

The one R word that the entire Autism community can agree on is Resentment. There is plenty of that to go around and then some.

Say this or something like this:

I use words to uplift myself and my child. Together we define what words are right for our family. I am respectful of the words others use to define themselves, but I value my child's opinion on this above all others.

CHAPTER
27
Parting with Friends

A t some point in your Autism-filled journey, you are going to discover that not everyone is suited to go on this journey with you. It might be a friend who just can't seem to understand that your new schedule doesn't have as much time for them. It could be a family member who can't get hold of the idea that their endless, uninformed, but well-meaning suggestions aren't helping anyone. It could be an employer who doesn't value your time or your talents enough to give you the flexibility you need to make your life work. The truth is that you may not have the time or energy to keep investing in these relationships. If you find yourself having to take time away from your family to do things that don't point you further in the direction of where your moral compass is heading…give yourself permission to say goodbye.

If your reaction to saying goodbye is relief, then you have absolutely done the right thing. It feels harsh. You may have friends or family who tell you that you are being selfish, hardheaded, hard-hearted. They may question you, "What has happened to you? Who have you become?"

You've become a parent of an individual on the Autism Spectrum. You have things on your to-do list that you never could have imagined before. You don't have time to hold everyone's hand anymore or to be all things to all people. Your child needs help and support, you need help and support, and anything that isn't helpful and supporting is like a big, fat weight in the lifeboat that is your life. It has to be thrown over the side or it could sink you all. Harsh? Yes. But it's true.

Think of it this way. If you had a friend and their child was in a car accident and broke both their legs, what would happen?. The child would need hours of therapy to be able to walk again. Your friend would be very busy for quite a while. Would you expect them to still make time for you and the fun things you used to do? No. Would you expect them to continue solving your problems? Nope. In short, would you expect them to put up with the behavior you have been putting up with? No. You would think that they were entitled to space and support and you would want to protect them from people who put too many expectations on them. You would be furious with anyone who even intimated that they were behaving selfishly for putting their child's needs first. Right? Autism is not two broken legs. But it is serious business that requires serious interventions. Without those interventions the child is not going to make as much progress. You can try to explain that to people, but if they don't get it, you can't make it your life's work to convert them. You need to save that energy for your child and your family. If the friends and family truly want to be helpful, they will change their behavior and be supportive. If they don't, wish them well and move on. For every friend or family member you lose, you will find twenty special needs parents who will gladly stand shoulder-to-shoulder with you while you take care of everything you have to take care of.

Don't be afraid to tell friends and family how they can help. I famously said to my mom, "Mom, I need your support or your silence. I don't have the bandwidth for anything else." That was a tough little moment. I thought my mother was going to inhale her lips. It took her a little minute, but she got on board and became one of my best supports while she was still alive.

There were other people I just stopped talking to. I wish I could say I missed them. I was busy enough that I really didn't register the loss of their presence in my life.

Be willing to shove people out of your lifeboat if they are threatening to sink the whole ship.

Say this or something like this:

I am allowed to have boundaries. I deserve to be surrounded by people who recognize the commitment I have made to my child and its importance to my current life. I am allowed to let go of friends, family, and colleagues who don't understand my priorities. I am strong enough to be steadfast in my desire to help my child.

CHAPTER
28
Holidays

"**A**ren't Holidays great?" said the person you used to be before you became a parent of an individual with an Autism diagnosis.

"No, they are a sensory nightmare," says the person you are now.

Maybe the truth is somewhere in between. Here is the thing about Holidays. They come with expectations. All of us have an idea in our heads what we want the holiday to be like. There's a perfect Norman Rockwell-esque image in our heads that features love, laughter, fabulous food that doesn't cause indigestion, thunder thighs, or a sugar haze but of course creates a ubiquitous feeling of belonging. Our vision has no room for discomfort; it's chock-full of inner peace. Now that we have a child on the spectrum, it seems clear that the picture will never happen. Darn Autism! Thanks to Autism, even unwrapping presents is a sensory-overloading experience that leads to tears and hysteria. It's easy to get caught in the emotional succubus of self-pity.

But just for a moment, I want you to think realistically about holidays in general. Even without Autism, they can be pretty trying. Someone invariably has a meltdown even without Autism. People get crabby, everybody gets a little thrown off. We think it's going to be great, but it usually isn't. Sure, there are elements that are great, so that's what we need to hold on to. What part of the perfect holiday do you want to invest in? Who else can you get excited about that element of the holiday? You like the decorating but not the cooking? Invite the friend over who loves to decorate and get a prefab meal from your local grocery store. You don't have to do it all.

Holidays can bring on sensory overload to anyone. Having a person on the spectrum in your family just makes it crystal clear and motivates you to consider editing the sensory elements. That is a good thing. For everyone. So decide what the important parts of your holiday are, focus on those, and edit everything else. This is one of the gifts of Autism. It encourages you to think with sanity and appreciate the pure forms of joy instead of wading through a glut of holiday overload and hoping to strike on a feeling we remember from the past.

Get organized, way in advance if possible. I like to ask my family every year what one thing they are looking forward to that really makes it feel like the holiday to them. When my son was younger and couldn't tell me, I showed him pictures of things we had done the year before and watched his reactions. If we are going to edit the Holiday, let's make sure we leave the stuff in that is really important. It's important not to assume.

I love going to the mall and seeing all the decorations and seeing the shoppers. I don't like being at the mall if I have to buy something. UGH, the lines are long! It loses all the fun for me. So I buy online and then visit the mall for a short while to take in the atmosphere!

I love having the house decked out for the holidays—whether it is Halloween, Christmas, or Saint Patrick's Day. My husband and son enjoy decorating for ten minutes, and then they are done. So I decorate and put things aside for them and let them come in and finish for ten minutes. Everyone is happy.

Food is a big part of Holidays. For some inexplicable reason, people want to serve meals at weird times. This is a red flag for me. It means someone is going to have a meltdown. Let me ask you something. Have you ever skipped lunch to power through something and didn't eat until 3 in the afternoon? How'd that work for you? Were you crabby? Or, at the very least, less able to cope? It's not ideal, right? So why do people invite you for Thanksgiving Dinner at 3 PM? Someone invariably has a meltdown; usually it is not the person on the spectrum, but we do it anyway. It's like this insane dance people insist on doing! Here is my solution. If you are invited to dinner at a weird time, feed your child and yourself at the normal time. You can do this at home or take an "antipasto tray" with enough to share with everyone. Ignore people who tell you you're spoiling your dinner. Then at dinner time, eat less. Don't expect your child to eat anything. They might, or they might take in more of the social situation; both are okay.

There is always someone who will have a very outspoken opinion of what you and your child are eating or not eating. Remember our mantra? Other people's opinion of my parenting is none of my business! This extends to food and holidays. I invite you to decide how you will handle this well in advance.

Some people just use a witty comeback:

"Thank you, Aunt Martha, but he hasn't starved yet, I think he's okay!"

Others simply are prepared to change the subject:

"Aunt Martha, I heard you had cataract surgery. What was that like? A guy I work with is talking about having that surgery, so I want to know all!"

She will be so busy telling you every detail she won't have time to notice what your kid is eating.

For super hardcore people, you can consider sending a brief note in advance.

> *Dear Aunt Martha,*
> *We are really looking forward to seeing you at Thanksgiving. I just wanted to let you know that we are working on a new intervention with Jason,*

and our therapy team has asked that we not talk to him about his food. I know it's kind of odd, but if you have any questions about Jason's food or the way he's eating/not eating, could you talk to me or Mike when Jason isn't around? Thank you for continuing to support us and our family as we help Jason. It has meant so much to us.

Aunt Martha may not be able to keep her pie hole shut, but you will be justified in being upset with her if she doesn't.

If you are spending any portion of a holiday at someone else's house, make sure to identify a sensory-friendly zone you can retreat to with your child. It might be a walk around the block, the garage, or a bathroom far from everyone. Retreat there whenever it appears your child is even mildly starting to escalate. Everyone is going to have thoughts and feelings about this. I encourage you to let them and not even attempt to "make it okay" for everyone. If you need to have a code word or phrase that is just for your family, use the key word to signal we are going to step aside and take a moment. Everyone should use this strategy in their lives; the world would be a better place. But we certainly can do this for our kids.

Don't be afraid to change the rules and create new traditions that suit your family's unique needs. When my son was little, we weren't giving him any sugar of artificial colors. We had no idea what we were going to do for Halloween. It's such a candy-intensive holiday, and back then there were no turquoise pumpkins or organic candies colored with beet juice! We decided to take the parts of the holiday we wanted and to rewrite the rest of the script. We played up the dressing up in costume. Every day in the month of October, we would put the costume on and take pictures. By the way, I really recommend this. It helped him to get used to the costume and it meant I got pictures. If you wait and try to do the pictures on Halloween…Good luck to you. I could never get that to work. It also means you don't have to care if the whole costume stays on during the festivities. My son was Spock from *Star Trek* one year. I don't think he went five feet before an ear came off. Then it was the belt, then the wig. Who cared, he was having fun and I already had pictures! The other thing we did was create a LEGO Fairy. We told our son that the LEGO Fairy LOVES candy and that at the end of Halloween, if he would put all his candy on the dining room table, the LEGO Fairy would come and take it and leave him a LEGO kit. The more candy, the bigger the LEGO. Suddenly my son was thrilled to trick or treat and get candy, but he didn't want to eat a single piece of it! After telling this story, I know other families that have created a Barbie Fairy, A Thomas the Tank Engine Fairy, and many more. Where did the candy go? The dentists in our area would collect candy to send to the troops. My son eats candy now, but it's not a big deal to him. It's not wrapped in a childhood memory for him, so it's not unusual for him to enjoy one piece and say that's enough for him.

I encourage you to rewrite your holidays. Be creative and make it work for you. Don't expect a perfect holiday, and you might find a holiday that is filled with enough elements to make you happy.

Say this or something like this:

This holiday is an opportunity for me to slow down and be present. I do not have to live up to any ideal picture in my head or someone else's head. I am grateful to spend this holiday with my child and to view its rituals through their eyes. I can feel free to release all expectations and allow myself to experience whatever happens, knowing that it will be okay.

CHAPTER
29
Social Skills

A deficit in social skills is a core part of an Autism Spectrum Diagnosis, but it can present itself in many ways. Not being able to make eye contact is considered a social deficit. Not being able to consider another's point of view is considered a social deficit. Of course, the irony is that society decides what social skills are necessary, so it's arbitrary. What is acceptable in 2022 isn't close to what was acceptable in 1920. Social Skills evolve with mankind. It is reasonable to argue that society will evolve and normalize somewhere within the realm of the Autism spectrum. It already has to some extent.

Some self-advocates and some parents of individuals with Autism will make the argument that we should not be teaching social skills to people with Autism; we should be teaching acceptance skills to neurotypical people. I'm all for teaching neurotypicals (including myself) how to be more flexible and accepting of alternate ways of thinking and being, but I don't agree that we shouldn't be teaching social skills. To me, that's like moving to China and deciding that you aren't going to learn Chinese. Why should you? English is a really great language for communicating. It's not the most popular language but it's a viable language and if people really want to communicate with you they should and will learn it. Learning Chinese would take a lot of effort on your part. Why should you have to? Let everybody else learn English. It's not a winning argument for me, but unfortunately some people feel that way. They feel that having to learn Chinese might change them. To me, learning Chinese doesn't mean you unlearn English. You will always be able to speak English, but once you know Chinese, you have options. You are no longer held back by an inability to communicate. You get to choose how and when you communicate. I feel the same way about teaching social skills. I'm all for it, but I'm just very fussy about how it is taught. I struggle with the concept of putting a bunch of people with social skills deficits in a room together and not ever having them interact with folks who don't have social skills deficits. It hurts my head. Social Skills classes may start in a sheltered environment but then should quickly move to settings that feature real interactions with people who do not have social skills deficits. Color me crazy.

If you are looking for a social skills class for your child, consider asking these questions:

1. Are these classes inclusive?
2. What is the ratio?

3. What kinds of activities do you do?

4. Is there peer mentoring?

5. Is there video modeling?

6. How will my child get feedback on their social skills?

Some great social skills classes are labeled other things. Drama and Improv classes are great social skills classes. Dr. Temple Grandin and Dr. Kerry Magro, two of the world's most renowned speakers, both on the spectrum, credit acting and theater classes with helping them overcome social skills issues.

I want to be sensitive about masking. Many self-advocates feel that they are expected to mask who they are by learning to play the rules of social interaction the way neurotypicals do. As a former teacher, I feel strongly that we should always give individuals the opportunity to learn things but give them the option of using their skills in the way they choose to. Sometimes that means building into the lessons an understanding of an individual's right to break the rule being taught. This is one of the hallmark differences between good-quality ABA and imposters. Good-quality ABA taught my son how to have boundaries, how to opt out of situations that were uncomfortable, and how to say no when he chose to do so. It also taught him how to connect with people who think differently and how to deal with the frustration of having to change the way he would like to communicate when it is not being received.

I think teaching skills is generally a positive thing, but we certainly have to be vigilant in making sure the teaching methods are individualized, empathetic, and not ableist in nature.

Say this or something like this:

Social Skills allow my child to have friends and a sense of community. I will help my child learn social skills, but I will listen to their needs in regards to social situations. I will focus on what is meaningful to them.

CHAPTER

◄ 30 ►

Taking Advice

Everybody has advice for you. Now, with the internet, you can't get away from it. How are you supposed to know what to do? Research is important. I like to ask myself the following questions:

1. *Is this advice coming from someone who has done what they are telling me to do? How did it turn out for them? Is there proof?*

   I think we all appreciate it when people who don't have children give parenting advice. That is some high comedy right there! Or when the fattest person at the table starts giving diet advice! Yeah, they may know more about dieting than anyone at the table, but if they couldn't figure it out, do you really want to take their advice? When I want parenting advice, I go to the parents who have kids that I want my child to be like. I look for happy kids who feel like they have a right to their own opinion and who aren't afraid to be different. I want to talk to the parents of those kids.

2. *Is there scientific evidence to back up this advice? Has anyone done a study on it? How big was the study? Is there more than one study?*

 I believe in innovation, but I don't believe in making my child a test case for something that has not already shown promise.

I believe in supporting research, and my son participated in several studies, but we always followed the motto of "do no harm."

Always do a gut check. Does this advice feel right to me? If it doesn't, I'm out. I don't care whom it is coming from. Sometimes it is hard to distinguish between fear and your gut saying no. Fear for me is immobilizing. When I get stuck, I know it is fear. When it is fear, I have to do work and figure out what it is I am afraid of. When my gut says no, I have no problem listening and moving away from whatever is pushing my buttons.

Say this or something like this:

I am a smart parent. I do my research. I follow the science. I check my gut and I am no one's fool.

CHAPTER
31
The Cliff, Adulthood & Employment

If you're paying attention, you will know that I have only a smidge of experience being a parent of an adult on the Autism Spectrum ... so realistically, I should just sit down and keep quiet. Originally, I left this chapter out of the book, but it kept poking me. I kept thinking of all the parents out there who have been left out because their kids were diagnosed before the turn of the century, the "dark ages" of Autism. These are the parents we owe everything to. They are the ones who made it work before there were sensory-friendly shirts or Broadway shows. They survived school settings, sometimes without IEPs and without IDEA. These people are the toughest people on the planet, and I couldn't leave them out. Not when I have information, and I do.

Let's talk about "The Cliff." This is what we call the period of time when an individual ages out of their school services. In different states, this can mean different things. It could mean eighteen, twenty-one, twenty-four, or twenty-eight years of age. It could be based on skill level or which way the political wind is blowing. It's been dubbed "The Cliff" by the parents who have gone through it and who describe the terrifying feeling of freefalling with no net in site. The cliff is not an urban myth; it's real and it's terrifying. Each year there are more services and programs becoming available in more places, but there still aren't enough.

Here is what I know about the cliff:

It's never too early to plan for it. Start now, looking at what is available in your area. It doesn't matter what age your child is; go tour some of these places and programs. It's either going to give you hope and have you start a relationship with the people who run it—it's never too early to help them raise money and awareness—OR it is going to kick you in the butt and make you realize that the program you want for your kid doesn't exist yet. Hello, motivation! How do I know this?

For over ten years, I have covered every story I can find of programs that help adults on the spectrum. Guess what they all have in common? A parent who got worried because the thing they needed for their child when their child became an adult didn't exist.

Case in point:

Thorkil Sonne, the amazing Dad who knew that his son wasn't going to be looked at for work in the tech field despite being a genius if he didn't do something, change something. Thorkil created a program called Specialisterne.[7] He partners with a business or corporation and trains people on the spectrum to work in tech jobs for that company. The company gets amazing, skilled employees who are awesome, conscientious, punctual, and hard-working. Thorkil's programs have helped hundreds of individuals get quality jobs, but he started it because he wanted to help one person: his son.

Extraordinary Ventures[8] was started by a group of parents whose children had been involved in the TEEACH program. When they aged out of the system, there wasn't anything for them. The parents got together and created a conglomerate of five businesses that employ individuals with special needs. It trains them and keeps them employed.

Picasso Einstein[9] was started by two parents who wanted to make sure that entrepreneurship was available for their kids. They created a curriculum for individuals on the spectrum and their parents to help navigate the waters of being a business owner.

7. "Welcome to Specialisterne." Specialisterne USA. Accessed October 10, 2021. https://www.us.specialisterne.com/.

8. "Who We Are • Extraordinary Ventures," Extraordinary Ventures, accessed October 10, 2021, https://www.extraordinaryventures.org/about-us/.

9. "Think Differently: Picasso Einstein," PicassoEinstein, accessed October 10, 2021, https://www.piceinworks.com/.

These are just a handful of the many amazing stories that are out there. You have to look in your area to see what is available. You may be lucky; the perfect thing may exist right in your backyard. If it doesn't, the question becomes, "What would the perfect thing look like?" Once you've answered that question, you might find yourself dreaming about making it a reality. Congratulations. You've been chosen to do something amazing that will not only change the world for your child but for countless others. I wish you the best of luck, and I'm happy to help you anyway I can. At the very least, I can't wait to have you tell your story on *Autism Live!*

In the course of writing this book, my son grew up. He got his first real job with a real paycheck. I don't even have the words to describe what this has meant to him. It has been so freeing for him to work a job, do it well, make his own money, and decide how he wants to spend it. It has been life-changing.

My dear friend Joanne Lara, from Autism Works Now, drilled it into my head for years that everyone deserves the dignity of a job. I didn't believe her at first. I thought there might be some people who would be too overwhelmed by a job's demands. This is short-sighted thinking. What I like to call stinking thinking. It assumes there is no job with fewer demands and that the individual can't learn to overcome stress. They are both false premises that prevent people from working. Joanne was and will always be right: "Everyone deserves a seat at the table! And that means a J-O-B!"

As a group of parents, we need to plan for our kids to work. Everything we do needs to project to the world that this is our intent and expectation. We need to ask them what they want to be when they grow up. We need to teach them job skills alongside life skills. Here's the good news: it's not all on you!

Make your child's school do some of the heavy lifting. In the United States, if your child has a diagnosis of ASD, they qualify for an IEP. If they have an IEP, they also have the legal right to an ITP. A what? An IPT is an Individual Transition Plan. It is the very thing that is supposed to prevent the cliff! An ITP has to be created and implemented by a student's sixteenth birthday. Some states require this even earlier, at fourteen. An ITP is meant to address three separate areas:

1. Where the individual will live after they transition out of school.
2. Who will be the individual's support system and how will they maintain a "community?"
3. Where and how the individual will work?

Isn't that great? Isn't that wonderful? Doesn't it seem like there should be a parade? Here's the problem. Most schools are very inexperienced at implementing ITPs, so they don't really highlight it to parents. Often parents are oblivious to the entire ITP process! Don't be oblivious; ask questions. Ask to know what they have planned. Push the school to take your teen's ITP seriously. If more parents pushed schools to provide solid ITPs, it is reasonable to think there would be some far-reaching benefits:

- Students would make more progress toward life-time goals
- The "cliff" might be less scary
- Schools would get better at writing and implementing ITPs

Often schools will arrange internships to help a student gain job skills. This is a great way to get your teen/adult excited about being employed. Utilize all the resources the school has and then fill in what you can't get from them. This is a more practical plan than trying to do it on your own.

You can also talk to your state or county office of rehabilitation. I have seen parents get everything from funding for college or trade schools, to internships, to jobs! It's worthwhile to reach out to them and see what is possible.

Our teens and adults deserve the right to work. We need to prepare them and we need to prepare the world! Don't be mistaken; this is the new revolution!

Say this or something like this:

My child will be a productive member of the work force; it is their right. My child deserves the right to work, and I will help them to learn skills to make this a reality.

Resources

Wrong Planet

https://wrongplanet.net/

CHAPTER
32

Other People's Opinion of My Parenting Is None of My Business

As a parent of an individual diagnosed with Autism, I have had the opportunity to practice many new skills on a daily basis. One of the greatest things I have learned is that "Other People's Opinion of My Parenting is None of My Business"—think about that for a moment. Read it back and then take a deep breath. This is the truth, and it is the road to forgiveness, sanity, and a happier place in the sun.

Notice that it doesn't say, "I'm sure no one's talking about me or my kid, or the way I feed/dress/discipline/ raise/nurture/look at my child." Yeah...it doesn't say that, 'cause we all know that's not true. Everybody has an opinion! We can't change that, no matter what we do. In fact, there is no possibility that we could ever make everyone (*or even anyone*) happy with all of our parenting choices even if we devoted our every waking moment to it.

Stop and try to visualize what you would have to do to make the biggest current pain in your ass happy. I'm talking about the person whose voice you hear most often in your head. What would you have to do to make that person happy with your parenting? If you can, I want you to close your eyes for a second and picture everything you would have to do to make them happy. What would you have to give up to live the way this person thinks you should? What would you lose? And in the end, would they really be happy? Would you? Would your CHILD be happy? Is there any scenario in which you can picture your pain in the ass being happy while you are also happy and living the priorities that you hold closest? No? It's not *possible*, is it? Wow! Isn't it freeing to realize it can't be done?

It's not possible, so we can let it GO! Once we let it go, we get to do what we want to do, what makes sense, and what we have decided to do based on our needs, our kid's needs, and what we feel is right.

The great thing about this mindset is that is allows you to let go of the resentment of thinking, "They don't get it."

Truth Alert!

They don't get it! Nobody but you understands all that you have going on and all that you have to deal with. NOBODY!

Sure, other parents of individuals on the spectrum and other special needs parents have an understanding of what you are going through, but our kids are different, and our circumstances are different. Nobody but you knows what goes on in your house at 3 AM, so no one else's opinion is really valid anyway!

Anybody who is judging you is doing so with limited information...which, if you think about it, kind of makes them stupid. Honestly, if you said to me, "Do you think I should spend $300 on a dog?" The only sane response would be to say, "I don't know," and ask a bunch of questions: "Can you afford $300? Are you prepared to have the responsibility of having a dog? Are you allowed to have a dog where you live? Dogs live for a long time; are you prepared for the sacrifices and responsibilities that dog ownership brings?" I can think of hundreds of more questions that would be appropriate. Anything less than having those answers and I would have a truly uninformed opinion.

An uninformed opinion is what you are going to encounter over and over again as a parent in the world of Autism. Recognize it when you see it and school yourself to look the other way. You don't have to fix it. You are under no obligation to school the numbnut who offers their opinion as if it is the world's greatest gift when it is actually a turd in a punch bowl. It just isn't your business.

It has nothing to do with you and you aren't attached to it. It takes practice to get this mindset working.

Your mind will sometimes wonder if maybe they are right and you are wrong. Ask yourself this: This person giving advice, are they someone you would trust to leave your child with for a week, with no contact from you? If your answer is not an immediate yes, without reservations...then don't allow their opinion of you or your child another moment in your head. Sure, listen to advice and suggestions, but then freely weigh them on what you think and make the decision for yourself.

When it gets tough, say this, or something like this, to yourself...

Other people's opinion of my parenting is none of my business. I know what path I am on. I am making decisions based on what is good for my child today and in the long run. I am informed and involved in my child's growth and development. I take in information and I decide what is best for my child and for our family. I am strong and loving. I am a good parent.

Make it your mantra, sing it to a Disney theme song. Get it in your head, your heart, and your DNA. You've got this! Be proud! Other People's Opinion of my Parenting is none of my business!

A COVID ADDENDUM

Each and every one of us and our kids has been affected by COVID-19. It has not affected everyone the same way, so let's break it down first by age:

Children Waiting for Diagnosis

Getting a diagnosis is hard enough in normal times; in the pandemic it has been even worse. If you have been forced to wait for a diagnosis, do everything you can to speed up the process, but don't delay services. This means getting on every waiting list you can for a diagnosis and calling regularly to see if there are any cancellations that would allow you to come in sooner. Be so nice that the person on the phone starts rooting for you. While you are waiting, assume you will get a diagnosis and see if you can get on a waiting list to start quality ABA services. Some providers won't put you on the list until you have the diagnosis. You didn't hear this from me, but some parents have been known to tell a white lie, that they have the diagnosis but are waiting for the report, just to get on a list. I didn't say it. What you don't want to happen is to wait six months for a diagnosis and then get on a list for ABA services and wait six more months! Early intervention is key—so you can't afford to wait for anything. You need to get started. Go back and read the chapter about getting your child healthy. Start there. While you are doing that, I strongly advise you to take one of the RBT or BCAT training programs online. An RBT is a Registered Behavior Technician and a BCAT is a Board-Certified Autism Technician. These are the trainings people do to begin working with our kids. The trainings are offered online; some are even free or low-cost. You can pace your learning at your own speed. You will learn good stuff that will help your child now and in the future. If possible, ask other friends and family to do the training as well. This is what people used to do before ABA was funded by insurance. It's not easy, but it is possible. If the ABA waiting list is long, ask if they can give you parental training while you wait for services to start.

School-Aged Kids

I am hearing from parents that anxiety is at an all-time high with our school-aged kids. It makes sense, right? The rules have changed so many times! Are we wearing masks, and is it okay to be with friends? What are the rules today? It's frustrating for adults; how could it not be for kids known to have sensory issues? We have to be super patient and make it really fair for them. That means giving them the space to express themselves, lowering expectations when asking them to do something new, and giving meaningful rewards for attempts to do what is hard for them. They have to have an outlet for their feelings. Some families have given their kids drums to bang; others let their kids paint or run around a track at the park. Find what works for your family, but please give them an outlet!

Also, hold your school accountable. Ask for compensatory education for any services you didn't receive in the last two years. If it was in your child's IEP to get 300 minutes of OT and they only got 120, ask for compensatory education. They might give you more OT or they might write you a check to go get it elsewhere. Your child is owed those services. You have to ask.

Teens & Young Adults

This is a very important time to shore up your teen's or young adult's program. What do they need right now? Some will desperately need socialization opportunities to make up for what they lost. Others will need help leaving the house; they loved the isolation that came with COVID. Be careful; this is a tightrope. You can't go too fast or push too hard, but you also can't allow them to stagnate. Be kind to yourself and them. Take it slow, make it rewarding. Lure them out of their solitude with things that are unique and special to them. Listen to them with all your senses. If you go too fast, forgive yourself and then slow down. Go back to the last thing that was working and try that again.

It's important to remember that no matter the age or skill level, we all lost something and gained something else during COVID. Grieve what you need to and then quickly get back to supporting yourself and your family.

A word about masks. No matter how you feel about masks, there are some things to be considered. For our speech learners it is IMPERATIVE that we give them plenty of safe opportunities to see people's mouths moving while talking. They make clear masks; if you need to, buy them for everyone your child interacts with.

If you have an older kid, it is IMPERATIVE we work on diction while wearing masks—don't see this as anything other than an opportunity and jump on it. Make it fun, do it every day. If you don't, you might see your child regress, because if people don't understand them through the mask, then speech will not be rewarding. You might see regression or frustration. Instead, work on the diction and have a better result all the way around.

Say this or something like this to yourself:

We are survivors. We will continue to take one day at a time and face each challenge as it comes. We have learned to be flexible and adapt. We do not wait; we find the way. This is who we are.

MY FAVORITE RESOURCES

Podcasts

Autism Live

www.autism-live.com

A free and interactive podcast that seeks to provide information and inspiration to those on the spectrum and everyone who loves them.

Ask Dr. Doreen

www.autismnetwork.com

A free, interactive program featuring Autism expert Dr. Doreen Granpeesheh answering questions from viewers around the world.

Stories From the Spectrum

www.storiesforthespectrum.com

This podcast features segments designed, hosted, filmed, and produced by individuals on the spectrum.

The Brady Bunch of Autism

www.teafc.org

Matt Asner and Navah Paskowitz-Asner host this entertaining and informative program from The Ed Asner Family Center.

Funding & Grant Opportunities

United Healthcare Children's Foundation
http://www.uhccf.org/apply/

This 501I(3) non-profit charity gives grants up to $5,000 to help families gain access to medical-related services. You DO NOT have to have United Healthcare Coverage to apply, but there are other requirements. I have seen many families successfully get this grant for copays and other medical bills.

Autism Care Today!
http://www.act-today.org/

This non-profit organization helps families receive grant money for technology, equipment, therapies, copayment assistance, and more. Funds are limited, so take the time to write a personal letter where noted in the application.

Autism Speaks
https://www.autismspeaks.org/financial-autism-support

This is a comprehensive list of resources to help with all financial needs, including rent.

iTaalk
https://www.itaalk.org/grant-and-funding-source-list

This link is to a comprehensive list of funding sources that are both Autism and non-autism-specific.

KNOWAutism

https://know-autism.org/apply-for-assistance/
This organization provides funding for tuition and diagnostic assistance as well as special case items like summer camp.

Books About Autism

Granpeesheh, Doreen. *Evidence-Based Treatment for Children with Autism: The Card Model.* Oxford: Academic Press, 2014. The ABA for Autism Book.

Adams, Christina. *A Real Boy: A True Story of Autism, Early Intervention, and Recovery.* New York: Berkley Books, 2005. The book that made me believe.

Grandin, Temple, and Oliver Sacks. *Thinking in Pictures: And Other Reports from My Life with Autism.* New York: Vintage Books, 2020.

Grandin, Temple, and Richard Panek. *The Autistic Brain: Exploring the Strength of a Different Kind of Mind.* London: Rider Books, 2014.

Cutler, Eustacia. *A Thorn in My Pocket: Temple Grandin's Mother Tells the Family Story.* Arlington, TX: Future Horizons, 2016.

Rosaler, Maxine. *Queen for a Day: A Novel in Stories.* Encino, CA: Delphinium Books, Inc., 2019.

Baker, Jed. *Overcoming Anxiety in Children and Teens*. Arlington, TX: Future Horizons, Inc., 2015.

Lara, Joanne, and Susan Osborne. *Teaching Pre-Employment Skills to 14-17-Year-Olds: The Autism Works Now!® Method*. London: Jessica Kingsley Publishers, 2017.

Higashida, Naoki. *Fall down Seven Times, Get up Eight*. Hodder, 2018.

Books about Autism for Children & Teens

Peete, Robinson. *My Brother Charlie*, 2010. (A great book for siblings!)

L'Engle, Madeleine. *A Wrinkle in Time*. New Delhi: General Press, 2019. (This classic never mentions Autism, but reading it will create a backdrop to talk about many aspects of Autism.)

Books About Diet

Silberberg, Barrie. *The Autism & ADHD Diet: A Step-by-Step Guide to Hope and Healing* by Living Gluten Free and Casein Free (GFCF) and Other Interventions. Sourcebooks, 2009.

Matthews, Julie. *Nourishing Hope: Nutrition Intervention and Diet Guide for Healing Children*. Self-published, Healthful Living Media, 2007.

Lewis, Lisa S., et al. *Special Diets for Special Kids*. Future Horizons, Inc., 2011.

Seroussi, Karyn, and Lisa S. Lewis. *The Encyclopedia of Dietary Interventions for the Treatment of Autism and Related Disorders: The Essential Reference Guide for Parents and Physicians.* Sarpsborg Press, 2008.

Seroussi, Karyn. *Unraveling the Mystery of Autism and Pervasive Developmental Disorder: A Mother's Story of Research and Recovery.* Broadway Books, 2002.

Arts Resources

The Ed Asner Family Center
https://edasnerfamilycenter.org/
Provides free daily online classes as well as low-cost in-person classes, events and counseling! An amazing place with amazing resources!

Spectrum Laboratories
https://www.speclabs.org/
Amazing collaborative classes for teens and adults to identify and develop their artistic passion. Online and in-person classes.

Danimation Entertainment
https://danimationentertainment.com/
Workshops and classes, online and in person, taught by Dani Bowman, a brilliantly talented self-advocate.

The Art of Autism
https://the-art-of-autism.com/
Non-profit organization connecting artists to the community.

Autism Movement Therapy
https://www.autismmovementtherapy.com/
Dance movement program to connect the brain and body.

Exceptional Minds
https://exceptional-minds.org/
Animation, visual effects, and 3D digital gaming element classes and camps designed for individuals on the spectrum.

The Miracle Project
https://themiracleproject.org/
Acting, singing, and social skills classes. Online and in-person.

Support for Parents

TACA Parent Support Network
www.tacanow.org

Families for Early Autism Treatment (FEAT)
http://www.feat.org/

Autism Society of America
www.autism-society.org

Council of Parent Attorneys and Advocates
www.copaa.org

For Teens & Adults

Movie Night with Chelsea Darnell at The Ed Asner Family Center. FREE
https://www.facebook.com/groups/270577694019575

PEERS Social Skill Programs
https://www.semel.ucla.edu/peers

Social skills classes for teens and caregivers, online and in person.

Specialisterne
https://specialisterneusa.com/

Helping to employ and support employment for neurodiverse individuals.

Picasso Einstein Works
https://www.piceinworks.com/

Online classes to teach job and entrepreneurial skills.

Autism Works Now
http://autismworksnow.org/

Online and in-person classes to teach job readiness.

Online Learning and Enrichment

Khan Academy

https://www.khanacademy.org/

Free lessons for pre-K through high school and beyond. This is a great resource. Parents can take a class with their children, and it can be used to reteach, teach, or enrich.

ABCYA

https://www.abcya.com/

Tons of learning games and activities for learners K–6, curriculum guides and standards help caregivers choose appropriate content.

Go Noodle!

https://www.gonoodle.com/

Videos and activities that are educational, with music and dancing. There are two apps, GoNoodle Games and GoNoodle Videos. Both are free.

Amazing Educational Resources

http://www.amazingeducationalresources.com/

Just what the name suggests. Learn by age and topic to find tons of resources. All resources are NOT free. Proceed with caution.

Camp Discovery

Free Autism Language Learning App that builds language skills through fun game play. Perfect for car rides to and from therapies. Available from Apple Store and Google Play.

Toys That Support Learning & Growth

Autism Live's Annual Toy and Gift Guide
https://autism-live.com/ToyGuide

A free resource of gifts and toys broken down by age and area of skill development.

AUTISM LIVE'S 100 THINGS TO DO WITH YOUR KIDS

1. Read with/to your kids. Reading is fundamental! There is no age limit. Make it fun and interactive.
2. Act out what you read. Don't be afraid to be silly. Create voices. Feel free to move and get your children moving.
3. Draw pictures about what you read. Read a chapter and then draw pictures about the chapter you read. Show your kids what you drew and why, and ask them to show you what they drew.
4. Sing! Karaoke or acapella! Singing stimulates the vagus nerve, which lowers stress. Sing with your kids! Some cable companies have a karaoke channel. Disney Plus has great sing-alongs, but if you are saving money, you can find lots of free karaoke videos on YouTube.
5. Learn a new song from YouTube. Don't know too many songs? That's okay. Learn something new. Find a song your kids like and learn it with them. Learn all the words. Put some dance moves with it. Don't be afraid to take out your camera.
6. Start a band. Use pots, pans, and other household items to make instruments. Improvise or play along to an existing song.
7. Build a blanket fort. Use tables, chairs, and blankets to create a special hangout! Add pillows and favorite things to make it cozy and comfortable. This might be the perfect place to read with your kids, with a flashlight, of course. Don't worry about making a mess! No one is coming over anyway!
8. Build a pasta tower. This is a great STEM exercise. Put a variety of pasta (spaghetti, lasagna and penne are the best) and marshmallows on the table and have a contest to see who can build the highest tower.
9. Find a craft on Pinterest and do it. Don't worry about having it be perfect. Half the fun of doing a Pinterest craft is seeing

how differently it comes out. Search Pinterest fails and have a laugh!

10. Find a science experiment on Pinterest and do it. Pinterest is filled with science experiments you can do with your kids, using common household products.

11. Make a music video to your favorite song. The sky is the limit. Have your child pick the song and the story line of the video. Have a blast trying to capture their vision.

12. Make a short movie. It could be about anything. It could reenact their favorite scene from their favorite movie or be something they made up.

13. Learn a magic trick online. Here are five magic tricks you can teach even a small child. Let them perform their own show, just like the kids in the video! https://youtu.be/V2tDK9wfCYs

14. Learn a dance on YouTube. Personally I am a fan of the Phil Wright. He is a choreographer who does dance classes with families that are super fun. Watch his videos and learn the moves with your kids. There are several, but here is my favorite: https://www.youtube.com/watch?v=_zdv23bAINM

15. Make an obstacle course in your house and have each family member run the course!

16. Make a how-to video. Is your child good at something? Have them do a short explainer video to teach the rest of us.

17. Bake something, anything. Have your kids help, make it fun.

18. Play treasure hunt. Hide a treasure and give your kids clues where to find it!

19. Teach everyone how to do laundry. Make it fun! My friend Karen says: "We play Dry Cleaners. We clock in, register the laundry on our computer, process everything, and complain about the manager. It's all imaginary, so it's not like we literally use a computer program or anything, but both of my girls love this."

20. Take a class with your kids on www.KhanAcademy.org. This is

a free platform that has classes appropriate for pre-K through college. Register for a parent account and a student account. Take a class alongside your kiddo, and track their progress. Did I mention it's FREE!

21. Watch an opera and sing like the actors.
22. Play a board game! In fact, play all the board games you have, just not all at once!
23. Go for a walk. There's nothing quite like a walk around the block!
24. Play beauty parlor. Let's all do each other's hair and nails. Don't be sexist and leave the boys and men out. This is great fun for everyone.
25. Play School and let your kids be the teacher. Be a good student and learn whatever your child decides to teach.
26. Make your living room a bowling alley with water bottles as the pins. Bowling balls could be oranges, grapefruit, baseballs...The list is endless.
27. Turn anything into a competition. Who can make their bed the fastest, who can pick up the most toys in twenty seconds? Give prizes and awards.
28. Play tag inside. It's important to keep everyone moving. Tag can be super fun! If you don't have space to run safely, try it while crab-walking! It takes up more space, but it slows everybody down!
29. Visit the library virtually or in person. Use www.overdrive.com and the Meet Libby app and you can borrow digital books from your library for free!
30. Put on a show in your living room. Act out scenes from your favorite Disney movies.
31. Play FREEZE with your TV. Put it on something active like sports, dance, or exercise. Take turns pausing the TV and having everyone try to copy the frozen person on TV—hilarious!
32. Exercise with a workout video on YouTube or other social

media. There are so many exercise videos online; there is something for everyone.

33. Call a family member or friend on Facetime! Have some set topics and questions to help foster conversations.

34. Have your child help make lunch or dinner. Make it fun for them and compliment them on being a good helper.

35. Do yardwork. This may not seem like fun, but it is actually really good for our kids to use their big muscles, get some sunshine and fresh air, and feel like they are accomplishing something. Clear weeds and leaves, plant seeds and flowers, dig up flower beds, etc. It will help tire them out so they will sleep better.

36. Put on music, hook up the hose and wash your car!

37. Institute a ten-minute cleaning fest where everyone cleans, puts things away, dusts, and vacuums for ten minutes. Make it fun, be silly!

38. Make race cars with LEGOS or recyclables and race them. https://www.youtube.com/watch?v=bbTHpA4ENYc

39. Make puppets out of old socks. We love the Smarty videos. Here is the one teaching how to make a sock puppet: https://www.youtube.com/watch?v=3AuOulSOYCw

40. Do a puppet show. Move the couch out, get behind it, and do a show with your kids. Record it on your phone so they can see it.

41. Watch a classic movie with your child. Now is a great time to introduce your kids to all the classic movies you loved as a kid. Have they seen all the things on this list? Many are available on streaming services. Here's a great starter list from Common Sense Media, that includes age ratings, and info about what might be upsetting to different kids: https://www.commonsensemedia.org/lists/50-movies-all-kids-should-watch-before-theyre-12

42. Get the crayons out and draw what you are feeling. Art is a great outlet for what we are feeling!

43. Take an online typing class with your kids. Here are ratings for some that are free! https://www.lifewire.com/free-typing-lessons-1356656

44. Turn a laundry basket into a race car. Push your child around in it. Then put toys or laundry in it and have them push it around. This is good exercise and mad fun!!

45. Play "The Floor is Lava" with your kids. Make sure to participate and supervise. The rules: The floor is pretend lava, so you can't step on it. You can start by filling the room with dining room chairs that help you get around the room. Use caution. Be safe, but this is great fun.

46. Do art projects with handprint and footprints. Turn your child's foot into a Disney Princess https://www.pinterest.com/pin/462322717976856091/ or a Marvel SuperHero: https://www.pinterest.com/pin/461548661801337180/

47. Take an online yoga class with your kids. There are so many on YouTube! Here is just one: https://www.youtube.com/watch?v=X655B4ISakg

48. Learn Tai Chi with your kids. Here is a video with ten easy-to-learn Tai Chi movements you can do with your kids! https://www.youtube.com/watch?v=vHBR5MZmEsY

49. Make a balance beam out of tape on your living room floor. Practice walking across it with different silly walks, and don't fall off.

50. Dress up in costumes, either Halloween costumes or make your own silly costumes. Take pictures.

51. Play a card game.

52. Go through your toy box/bin and find toys you haven't played with in a while, and find new ways to play with them. For example, make a stop motion video with old figures.

53. Build something unique out of LEGOS or other construction toys.

54. See who can make the highest house of cards

55. Have a video game tournament.
56. Do the Hokey Pokey!
57. Go for a drive and listen to a book on tape.
58. Watch educational programing for all ages on PBS.
59. Watch an old-fashioned musical and get up and perform with it.
60. Do silly tongue twisters. Here are fifty to get you started: https://www.engvid.com/english-resource/50-tongue-twisters-improve%20pronunciation/
61. Draw faces on your hands, and do a puppet show. This doesn't have to be rocket science. Use a nonpermanent marker, draw eyes and a face on your hand, and let the fun ensue.
62. Draw faces on your toes. Sing a song. Make a video.
63. Teach your child how to load or unload the dishwasher. Make it fun. Then challenge them to always put their dishes in the dishwasher as soon as they are done eating! Will they remember every time? Create an easy reward! Three meals per day—for every time you remember to put your dishes in the dishwasher, you get five extra minutes of reading time at night!
64. Put wax paper under your feet and "skate" around the room. Be careful! This can get pretty slippery!
65. Make a robot out of stuff lying around the house.
66. Play a game where you take small amounts of fragrant things from around the house, in the fridge, and in your yard. Put them in separate cups, bowls, or glasses. Take turns blindfolding your kids and have them guess what they are smelling.
67. Make mud, play in it, and make old-fashioned mud pies.
68. Make and dress your own paper dolls. There are plenty of sites to help you.
69. Play restaurant. Someone is the cook, someone is the waiter, someone is the customer. Go from ordering to paying; your kids will love it.

70. Get out your Christmas lights and hang them with your kids, wherever it makes you happy.
71. Make a collage with your kids using recycled materials.
72. Have your kids make a cooking show! Record it!
73. Play follow the leader.
74. Play Hot/Cold. Hide an agreed-upon item somewhere in the house. Start looking for it; the person who did it says "Cold" when you are not near the hidden item, "Warm" when you are getting closer, and "Hot" when you are really close. The person who finds the item gets to hide it the next time.
75. Rearrange the furniture with your kids. This is good gross motor activity.
76. Make masks out of paper plates. Here are some fun ones from Life as Mama: https://lifeasmama.com/20-easy-and-adorable-paper-plate-crafts/
77. Challenge older kids to make a video for YouTube about their favorite subject... even if it's video games.
78. See who can make the silliest face in a selfie. Have friends and family vote.
79. Play a video game as a family. We love to play Mario Kart as a family!
80. Do calisthenics as a family. Older kids can do push-ups, planks, and crunches but all kids can be encouraged to run in place, pretend swim, jump, and do toe touches!
81. Make a mural on the wall by taking old wrapping paper and hanging it facedown on the wall. Supervise your kids to only color or paint on the paper, not the wall. A fun thing to do is just draw shapes and lines, and have them color each shape a different color.
82. Make toilet paper tube art! Find ideas on Pinterest.
83. Play classical music and make up a story to go with the music. Later draw pictures together to illustrate the story you made up!

84. Make up a funny handshake with your kids. Be creative! Make it fun.

85. Make a crazy string sculpture in your house. Know where your scissors are before you start. Tie string to a doorknob and then tie it to something across the room. Zig-zag back and forth high and low until you run out of string. Practice trying to cross the room without touching the string. Make sure you take a picture before you cut your way out!

86. Teach your child to sew a button on.

87. Help your child to create a story or script. Act it out. Don't be afraid to be silly!

88. Pretend you are on a boat, on an airplane, in an elevator, at the zoo. PRETEND!

89. Pretend you are different animals, change frequently; take turns yelling out which animal to be.

90. Play "I Spy."

91. Make a fairy house with recycled materials.

92. Memorize a poem, scripture, monologue or speech, and perform it!

93. Pretend your kids are the parents and you are the kid! Let them order you around.

94. Play balloon volleyball. Blow up a balloon and try to keep it from touching the ground by hitting it into the air. Kids love this and don't realize it's good exercise!

95. Make soup out of all the fresh veggies you have in the fridge. Have your kids help you find ingredients for the soup.

96. Have a playdate! Invite a friend. Play a game together or read a story together.

97. Make popcorn the old-fashioned way.

98. Dance while vacuuming.

99. Play retail store. Make someone the cashier and someone the shopper. Have fun buying and selling your stuff! This teaches pre-employment skills!

100. Plant seeds, then water them. Watch them grow.

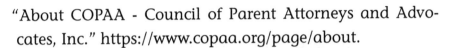

REFERENCES

"About COPAA - Council of Parent Attorneys and Advocates, Inc." https://www.copaa.org/page/about.

About Us. https://www.medmaps.org/about-us/.

Adams, Christina. *A Real Boy: A True Story of Autism, Early Intervention, and Recovery.* New York: Berkley Books, 2005.

"Autism Live." Autism Live. http://www.autism-live.com/.

Baker, Jed. *Overcoming Anxiety in Children and Teens.* Arlington, TX: Future Horizons, Inc., 2015.

"Board-Certified Behavior Analysts (BCBA)." Behavior Analyst Certification Board. https://www.bacb.com/bcba/.

"Books." The Work of Byron Katie https://thework.com/books/.

Cutler, Eustacia. *A Thorn in My Pocket: Temple Grandin's Mother Tells the Family Story.* Arlington, TX: Future Horizons, 2016.

"Family Resources." The Autism Community in Action (TACA). https://tacanow.org/family-resources/.

Grandin, Temple, and Oliver Sacks. *Thinking in Pictures: And Other Reports from My Life with Autism.* New York: Vintage Books, 2020.

Grandin, Temple, and Richard Panek. *The Autistic Brain: Exploring the Strength of a Different Kind of Mind.* London: Rider Books, 2014.

Grandin, Temple. *Calling All Minds: How to Think and Create like an Inventor.* New York, NY: Puffin Books, 2019.

Granpeesheh, Doreen. *Evidence-Based Treatment for Children with Autism: The Card Model.* Oxford: Academic Press, 2014.

Higashida, Naoki. *Fall down Seven Times, Get up Eight.* Hodder, 2018.

"Home." The Autism Community in Action (TACA). https://tacanow.org/.

"Individuals with Disabilities Education Act (IDEA)." Individuals with Disabilities Education Act. http://idea.ed.gov/.

Kingsley, Emily Perl. "Welcome to Holland." NDSS, July 24, 2020. https://www.ndss.org/lifespan/a-parents-perspective/.

LaMotte, Sandee. "Dirty Dozen 2021: View the List of Foods with the Most and Least Pesticides." CNN. Cable News Network, March 17, 2021. https://www.cnn.com/2021/03/17/health/dirty-dozen-foods-2021-wellness/index.html.

Lara, Joanne, and Susan Osborne. *Teaching Pre-Employment Skills to 14-17-Year-Olds: The Autism Works Now!® Method.* London: Jessica Kingsley Publishers, 2017.

L'Engle, Madeleine. *A Wrinkle in Time*. New Delhi: General Press, 2019.

Lewis, Lisa S. *Special Diets for Special Kids*. Arlington, TX: Future Horizons, Inc., 2011.

Matthews, Julie. *Nourishing Hope: Nutrition Intervention and Diet Guide for Healing Children*. Self-published, Healthful Living Media, 2007.

Peete, Robinson. *My Brother Charlie*, 2010.

Rosaler, Maxine. *Queen for a Day: A Novel in Stories*. Encino, CA: Delphinium Books, Inc., 2019.

Seroussi, Karyn, and Lisa S. Lewis. *The Encyclopedia of Dietary Interventions for the Treatment of Autism and Related Disorders: The Essential Reference Guide for Parents and Physicians*. Pennington, NJ: Sarpsborg Press, 2008.

Seroussi, Karyn. *Unraveling the Mystery of Autism and Pervasive Developmental Disorder: A Mother's Story of Research and Recovery*. New York: Broadway Books, 2002.

Silberberg, Barrie. *The Autism & ADHD Diet: A Step-by-Step Guide to Hope and Healing by Living Gluten Free and Casein Free (GFCF) and Other Interventions*. Naperville, IL: Sourcebooks, 2009.

"Think Differently: Picasso Einstein." PicassoEinstein. https://www.piceinworks.com/.

"Welcome to Holland," n.d.

"Welcome to Specialisterne." Specialisterne USA. https://www.us.specialisterne.com/.

"Who We Are • Extraordinary Ventures." Extraordinary Ventures. https://www.extraordinaryventures.org/about-us/.

"Wrightslaw." Wrightslaw Special Education Law and Advocacy. https://www.wrightslaw.com/.

Shannon Penrod was a teacher, actress, and award-winning stand-up comedienne when her life took a sharp left. Her world changed forever when her son was diagnosed with Autism at the age of 2 ½. Like many parents, Shannon and her husband began a mission of helping their son reach his highest potential. Their son is now a successful college student studying screenwriting! Shannon is committed to helping other families find their paths. Shannon is the President of The Autism Network, where she hosts the #1 rated Autism podcast *Autism Live*. She also hosts *Ask Dr. Doreen* and serves as Executive Producer for *Stories from the Spectrum*. Shannon frequently performs her award-winning comedy show, *The Autism Mamalogues*, and enjoys speaking to parents and professionals around the world. Her greatest privilege and joy in life is being her son's mother.

Temple Grandin for Kids!

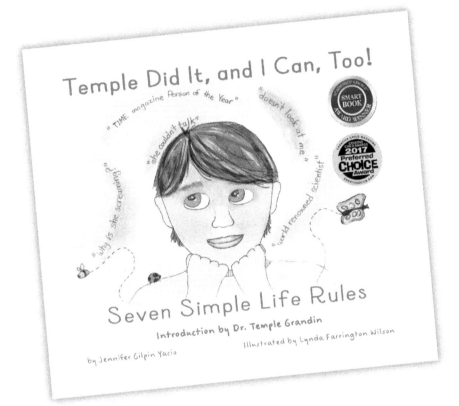

Temple Did It, and I Can, Too!

"TIME magazine Person of the Year"   "doesn't look at me"

"she couldn't talk"

"why is she screaming?"   "world renowned scientist"

SMART BOOK AWARD WINNER

CREATIVE CHILD MAGAZINE 2017 Preferred CHOICE Award

Seven Simple Life Rules

Introduction by Dr. Temple Grandin

Illustrated by Lynda Farrington Wilson

by Jennifer Gilpin Yacio

Here's a book that will help guide and inspire all kids to reach their full potential. *Temple Did It, and I Can, Too!* explains the obstacles Dr. Grandin faced while growing up, then gives seven rules she followed to overcome them and become a leading animal scientist.

FUTURE HORIZONS INC.   www.FHautism.com | 817•277•0727

CPSIA information can be obtained
at www.ICGtesting.com
Printed in the USA
JSHW042312220622
27203JS00002B/2